To My Parents

Reprinted 1979
by special arrangement with the University of California Press

OCTAGON BOOKS
A DIVISION OF FARRAR, STRAUS & GIROUX, INC.
19 Union Square West
New York, N.Y. 10003

Library of Congress Cataloging in Publication Data

Kleinman, Hyman H
    The religious sonnets of Dylan Thomas.

    Reprint of the ed. published by University of California Press,
Berkeley, which was issued as no. 13 of Perspectives in criticism.
    Bibliography: p.
    Includes index.
    1. Thomas, Dylan, 1914-1953—Criticism and interpretation. 2.
Sonnets, English—History and criticism. 3. Christian poetry,
English—History and criticism. I. Title. II. Series: Perspectives in
criticism; 13.
[PR6039.H52Z74   1979]   821'.9'12   78-26190
ISBN 0-374-94589-6

Manufactured by Braun-Brumfield, Inc.
Ann Arbor, Michigan
Printed in the United States of America

H. H. KLEINMAN

The Religious Sonnets
of Dylan Thomas

A STUDY IN IMAGERY AND MEANING

Why are not Sonnets made of thee?
—GEORGE HERBERT

OCTAGON BOOKS

A DIVISION OF FARRAR, STRAUS AND GIROUX

New York   1979

Preface

A POEM should mean as well as be. The sound of Dylan
Thomas's poems, especially when made palpable by his
voice, never left the reader or listener in doubt about the
existence of the poems. One heard with the hearing of
the ear, but what of understanding? The questions I
asked myself and the questions asked of me by my stu-
dents compelled certain answers. Those answers are in
this book. It is easy to talk above, below, or to the side
of a poem. Fortunately for me I have students who do
not believe in the tangentially prepositional approach
to poetry. They insist on an odyssey *into* a poem to dis-
cover its meaning, to marvel at its magic, to hear its
music. I have made that odyssey with them, aware of
the root meaning of exegesis: to lead out.

Exegesis has its dangers: chief among them pedantry,
weariness, and pretentiousness. I sought to avoid all
three by keeping before me the examples of the late
Professor John Livingston Lowes's graceful scholarship,
Professor Cleanth Brooks's critical vitality, and Profes-
sor William York Tindall's critical astringency. Long
ago it was Professor Tindall who taught me the creative
process of explication.

I have been careful to remember the complaint of
the Psalmist: "They laid to my charge things that I
knew not." I have not ascribed to Dylan Thomas an
erudition which he himself would have denied. When-

ever I drew comparisons, made analogies, and suggested similarities in themes and imagery between Thomas's sonnets and the works of other writers, I recalled the words of that erudite Welshman, Captain Fluellen: "There is a river in Macedon and there is also moreover a river in Monmouth . . . and there is salmons in both."

I have incurred many debts in the writing of this book, some of them very old ones. It is a pleasure to remind the following persons of my indebtedness to them for their acts of kindness: Miss Lillian Lang of the BBC made available to me a recorded and typewritten transcription of a 1946 broadcast in which Dylan Thomas had participated. Miss Jacqueline Castles and Miss Anne McCabe of the Columbia University Libraries made book borrowing a gracious ritual for many years. Mr. Robert Beach and his staff of the Union Theological Seminary Library extended numerous privileges and courtesies. The Reverend Father Kevin P. Fludd, S. J., of the library of Loyola Seminary, Shrub Oak, New York, offered his kind assistance. Mr. Eugene Magner of the Lockwood Memorial Library, Buffalo, New York, by his prompt arrangement of microfilm loans and his painstaking correspondence helped me immeasurably. Professor Robert M. Adams of Cornell University long ago gave me his encouragement. Professor Frank Caldiero of the Cooper Union Institute was generously thoughtful in presenting me with a recording of Dylan Thomas's remarks and readings at the Cooper Union Institute in 1950. Dr. Maurice Wohlgelernter of Yeshiva College and Mr. George Zimbel of Continental Village, New York, shared their special knowledge with me.

John H. Jennings and Grace Buzaljko of the University of California Press made themselves indispensable in the preparation of this book for publication. It is to Mrs. Buzaljko that I owe the present form of this book. Her long patience, tactful advice, gracious comments, and keen perception made her a necessary angel in manuscript editing. I learned from her that revision is not a chore but a pilgrimage in humility.

To my family I owe much. My daughter Nancy shared with me her knowledge of plankton to enable me to understand certain images in the sonnet sequence. My son Paul plundered his attic memory for an odd assortment of facts which I found invaluable. My wife knew, always, the very fine line between nagging and inspiration. This is really her book. She listened, commented, encouraged, and typed. She shared in pre-dawn doldrums and midnight doubts when crumpled papers and torn notes belied the possibility of this book's ever taking shape. The pen was in my hand, but it would not have moved across the page without her.

Whatever there is of illumination in this book I share with those who made it possible; what there is of obscurity or error is wholly mine.

All translations are my own except where otherwise indicated in the notes.

H.H.K.

Town of Cortlandt
Furnace Woods, New York

Acknowledgments

I AM GRATEFUL to the following persons and publishers for their kind permission to quote material from published and unpublished sources: New Directions for excerpts from the poems of Dylan Thomas: Copyright 1939, 1942, 1946 by New Directions. Copyright 1952, 1953 by Dylan Thomas. Copyright © 1957 by New Directions. Reprinted by permission of New Directions, Publishers. J. M. Dent and Sons, Ltd., for excerpts from the works of Dylan Thomas.

The Trustees of the British Museum for permission to reproduce an illustration from the manuscript collection of the British Museum; Cambridge University Press for excerpts from *The Mummy* by Sir Edgar Wallis Budge; Chatto and Windus, Ltd., and Miss Margaret Rickert, literary executrix of the estate of Edith Rickert, for selections from *Ancient English Christmas Carols,* collected and arranged by Edith Rickert; the Estate of Dylan Thomas, David Higham Associates, Ltd., and the Lockwood Memorial Library of the University of Buffalo for quotations from the manuscript notebooks of Dylan Thomas; Farrar, Strauss and Company, for an excerpt from *The Greater Trumps* by Charles Williams; Houghton Mifflin Company for several stanzas from the "Cherry-Tree Carol" in Child's *English and Scottish Popular Ballads,* edited by Helen Child Sargent and George Lyman Kittredge;

the Johns Hopkins University Press for quotations from *The Christ of Velázquez* by Miguel de Unamuno, translated by Eleanor Turnbull; Oxford University Press for quotations from *Poems of Gerard Manley Hopkins* and excerpts from *Religious Lyrics of the Fifteenth Century*, edited by Carleton Brown; Random House, Inc., for a line of verse from *Ulysses* by James Joyce, copyright 1914, 1918, and renewed 1942, 1946, by Nora Joseph Joyce; and Messrs. Rider and Company for a quotation and illustration from *The Mystic Mandrake* by C. J. S. Thompson.

Contents

Introduction

> Though it appear a little out of fashion,
> There is much care and valour in this Welshman.
>   *Henry V*, IV, 1, 85

DYLAN THOMAS has been called neo-romantic, surrealist, Freudian, apocalyptic. He has been described as a Welsh cultural irredentist, a Welsh folk poet, a Welsh prosodist. His poems have been attributed to the influence of bar and bethel, explicated in colleges, and read aloud in coffeehouses. He has been calumniated by epitaph writers and inscribed in the poets' martyrology by sentimentalists. Caught in his own myth of a latter-day Poe and Rimbaud, and exhausted by the bewildering sequence of motley and laurel, he died in a nightmare of confusion.

Dylan Thomas was a romantic poet, sharing with Keats the wonder of the senses and the bitter awareness that all flesh is grass. The epithet "apocalyptic" does not describe a poet who prophesied the end of the world in either bang or whimper; rather it suggests that Thomas's imagery was as mystical as the imagery of William Blake, Christopher Smart, St. John of the Revelation, and the authors of the Old Testament Apocrypha.

In a more formal and historical sense he was claimed as an apocalyptic poet, early in 1938, by a group of young English writers who called themselves the Apocalyptics. These young men issued a manifesto of liber-

1

ation from the influence of Eliot and Auden and created an apocalyptic pantheon in which they placed—in a rather arbitrary apotheosis—the following artists and writers: James Joyce, Franz Kafka, Vincent van Gogh, Pablo Picasso, Jacob Epstein, and Dylan Thomas. The writers of the Apocalypse, in turning from Eliot and Auden, sought a new heaven and a new earth and began a journey to the New Jerusalem. The group numbered more than four horsemen, among whom were Henry Treece, Nicholas Moore, J. F. Hendry, G. S. Fraser, and Tom Scott. But they soon rode off in different directions. Who could say where the New Jerusalem was?

I would hesitate to call Dylan Thomas a surrealist poet. His search for the reality beyond reality did not lead him to literary sources. He owed nothing to the ancestors of surrealism, Lautréamont and Apollinaire; nor to the later practitioners, Aragon, Breton, and Eluard. By the time Thomas had begun to write, the Continental surrealist wave had become a backwash across the Channel. Thomas was too consistent in his symbols, too controlled in his imagery, too disciplined in his prosody, and too mindful of his line count (so evident in his work sheets) to suggest automatic writing or an unobstructed flow of dream imagery. Nor is there any evidence to show that Thomas had participated in the revolt against rules, manners, morals, or metrics which is inherent in the surrealist movement. If his poems suggest the chaos of the unconscious, it is because Thomas knew—as Nietzsche did—that "one must have chaos to give birth to a dancing star."

The influence of Freud upon Thomas has been overemphasized. The source of this overemphasis lies, I believe, less in the poems than in Thomas's answer to an inquiry circulated among writers in 1934 by *New Verse* (number 11, October, 1934). The fourth question, in a series of six asked of the writer, was "Have you been influenced by Freud and how do you regard him?" To this question Thomas answered a simple "yes" and added the following statement:

Whatever is hidden should be made naked. To be stripped of darkness is to be clean, to strip of darkness is to make clean. Poetry, recording the stripping of the individual darkness, must inevitably cast light upon what has been hidden for too long and by so doing, make clean the naked exposure. Freud cast light on a little of the darkness he had exposed. Benefiting by the sight of the light and the knowledge of the hidden nakedness, poetry must drag further into the clean nakedness of light more even of the hidden causes than Freud could realize.

He might as well have substituted Milton's name for Freud's and quoted (with as much irrelevance to the question as that contained in his answer) Milton's lines from *Paradise Lost:*

. . . what in me is dark
Illumine, what is low raise and support; . . .
(Book I, ll. 20–23)

So much the rather thou, Celestial light,
Shine inward, and the mind through all her
    powers
Irradiate, there plant eyes, all mist from
    thence
Purge and disperse, that I may see and tell
Of things invisible to mortal sight.
(Book III, ll. 50–55)

I doubt that Thomas had much knowledge of Freud's work, nor do I believe that he used Freud's theories as a hydraulic device to dredge up symbols from his unconscious. Thomas's images came from his own substance, not from *The Interpretation of Dreams.*

Was Thomas a Welsh poet? He was Welsh by birth, not Welsh in tradition. Thomas, unlike Glendower,

3

spoke no Welsh; but like Glendower to Hotspur he could have exclaimed among contemporary English poets: "I can speak English as well as you." The belief that Thomas had derived a knowledge of Welsh prosody from Hopkins is not too sound. Thomas himself stated that he neither read nor spoke Welsh nor had any knowledge of Welsh prosody.

What may appear at first to be *cynghanedd* (Welsh metrical alliteration) or "consonant chime" in Thomas's poetry is really Anglo-Saxon alliteration. As long ago as the twelfth century a keen-eared Welshman, Giraldus Cambrensis, noted in his *Itinerary Through Wales* that the English as well as the Welsh

> employ this ornament of words [alliteration] in all exquisite compositions. . . . Nor can I believe that the English and Welsh, so different and adverse to each other, could designedly have agreed in the usage of this figure; but should rather suppose that it had grown habitual to both by long custom, as it pleases the ear by a transition from similar to similar sounds.

The influence of Hopkins on Thomas is reflected less specifically in Thomas's poems and more generally in Thomas's statements about Hopkins's influence. In 1946, in a BBC talk (later published) on Wilfred Owen, Thomas singled out four poets who, in his judgment, were profound influences on the poets who came after them. The four poets were Gerard Manley Hopkins, Wilfred Owen, the later Yeats, and T. S. Eliot.[1] In that same year, in another BBC program, Thomas claimed "that one of the profoundest influences on what we are now calling modern verse is Gerard Manley Hopkins."[2]

Dylan Thomas was not a Welsh irredentist nor a Welsh folklorist. The extent of his interest in Welsh culture never went beyond his brief editorship of the magazine *Wales*. The Welsh cultural renaissance was not so much his concern as it was that of Keidrych Rhys and Glyn Jones. Coal miners and distressed areas

4

were not themes for his poetry. His "loud hill of Wales" never echoed the plight of the Rhondda Valley; the slag heaps never defaced his "golden Glamorgan." There is little of Welsh folklore in his poetry except a reference to "sin-eater" in an early poem, and an oblique reference to a Laugharne worthy in "Over Sir John's Hill." We hear of Cadwallader's goats, Glendower's wizardry, Fluellen's leek, and Queen Mab's magic from a poet who knew the Avon better than the Tawe. Genuinely Cymric about Thomas were his name and his flair for rhetoric: the former he shared with a mythical character in *The Mabinogion*—Dylan, "son of the wave"; the latter he shared with the Druid bards.

II

Appraisals of Dylan Thomas's poetry in England ranged from Dame Edith Sitwell's generous praise to Sir Herbert Grierson's puzzled evaluation. Dame Edith wrote in 1936:

> Here, I said to myself, is a young man who has every likelihood of becoming a great poet, if only he will work hard enough at subduing his obscurity: I know of no young poet of our time whose poetic gifts are on such great lines.[3]

Sir Herbert noted in 1946 that

> With Mr. Dylan Thomas . . . the image comes first. When his barmy noddle's working prime— if one may quote Burns in such a connection— image after image boils up in it, to be fused and bent to his poetic purpose, though what that purpose is we can seldom discern through the tornado of wild and whirling words, violent metaphors, and Biblical allusions that envelops his fixed ideas about sex and sin, and death. Still he is a poet; he thinks in images, and to the imagination he appeals.[4]

Two contemporaries of Dylan Thomas, Henry Treece

and Francis Scarfe, combined critical insight and poetic sensibility to offer valuable conclusions. Treece, in his *Dylan Thomas* (1942), was systematic and detailed in his inventory of images, vocabulary, and influences; Scarfe, in his *Auden and After* (1942), was intuitive and analytical, dividing his essay between general comments and close reading.

In America two excellent full-length studies, of which I shall say more later, were written after Thomas's death: Elder Olson's *The Poetry of Dylan Thomas* and William York Tindall's *A Reader's Guide to Dylan Thomas*. Of the short reviews two penetrating appraisals of Thomas's work were written by Robert Lowell [5] and Leslie Fiedler,[6] who brought to their essays a warm appreciation, a detached perspective, a carefully detailed analysis of prosody, a sensitive perception of meaning, a praise of the poet's power, and a warning of his weakness. Mr. Lowell felt that "As a formal metrician, Wallace Stevens is the only living poet who can hold a candle to him." Mr. Fiedler observed that "the talent that can select words distinguished enough to bear the burden of the rime, is unrivalled, I think, since Arnaud Daniel." Mr. Lowell saw "a dazzling obscure writer who can be enjoyed without understanding," and Mr. Fiedler made the discovery that "there is in him an unmistakable wavering movement toward greater simplicity of tone, gestures, at least, toward a greater ease and certainty of communication." Aware with Mr. Lowell of Thomas's dazzling obscurity, Mr. Fiedler concluded with the following prophecy: ". . . but there are indications that he is preparing a style that, going beyond what dazzles and astonishes and suspends, will be able to encompass sensibilities and intuitions more mature and extensive, more self-confident and resolved."

Thomas's last volume, *In Country Sleep*, bears out Mr. Fiedler's prediction. The six poems in this collection revealed a poet who was certain in his craft, tender in his love, lyrical in his eloquence, and lucid in his meaning. I find the title poem, "In Country Sleep," as moving a statement of fatherhood in its hope and fear and anguish and love as Yeats's "Prayer For My Daughter" and Coleridge's "Frost at Midnight." Nor would I hesitate for a moment in dividing my admiration between Thomas's "Lament" and Yeats's "The Wild Old Wicked Man." The next poem, a birthday poem, marking as it does the "middle of the journey," is not so much an occasional poem as it is a dramatic pause for regret, recollection, and prophecy. I believe it is a poem as full of magic as Yeats's "Lines Written in Dejection" and as full in its range as Yeats's "The Circus Animals' Desertion." There is an echo of Cordelia's ". . . hold your hand in benediction o'er me" as Thomas asks his dying father's blessing in "Do Not Go Gentle Into That Good Night," exhorting him in imperative elegiacs not to submit to death quietly. "In the White Giant's Thigh" is set in a reflective nocturne recalling the song of the flesh now silent dust. And finally there is "Over Sir John's Hill" in which Thomas observed in terror and pity the ineluctable scheme of Nature in a riverscape of hawks and herons.

These six poems bore out in triumph the belief expressed by those who saw in Thomas not so much another "marvelous boy" but a fine, mature poet. The last poems framed the image of Dylan Thomas as others saw him and as he saw himself. The poems held for a moment a luminousness of hope at the same time that they sounded the echoes of doubt: they stand as an epitaph to an all too brief achievement.

III

The religious sonnets first appeared in the December, 1935, issue of *Life and Letters Today* as a group of seven sonnets under the title of "Poems for a Poem." Thomas had described his contribution in a letter to the editors as ". . . the first passage of what's going to be a very long poem indeed." He must have had some doubt about the editor's reception of his work in progress, for in the same letter he expressed the hope that the editors would "like it, despite its obscurity and incompleteness." [7] When the poem appeared in book form in *Twenty-five Poems* in 1936, three sonnets had been added. The publisher's statement on page vii of that volume informed the reader that "the last poem in the book contains the first ten sections of a work in progress." In his introduction to Dylan Thomas's *Letters to Vernon Watkins* (1957), Mr. Watkins recalls an evening at Thomas's home, where they had met to read their poems to each other: "Last of all," writes Mr. Watkins,

> he read the sonnet sequence, of which he had then written seven, beginning "Altar-wise by Owl-light in the Half-way House." He looked up on reading the last line: "On rose and icicle the ringing handprint." It was not many weeks before he added three more sonnets, on the Crucifixion, Egyptian burial, and the Resurrection, to the sequence. He intended to write more and make it a much longer work, but the sequence of ten sonnets was all he completed, and that is how it appears in his *Collected Poems*.[8]

That is all we know of the poem's genesis.

An interpretation of the first sonnet offered by Dame Edith Sitwell elicited from Thomas a vigorous disagreement which concluded with a statement that "this poem is a particular statement in a particular adventure . . ." [9] The interpretations of that particular incident in a particular adventure are varied.

Francis Scarfe, in his essay on Thomas in *Auden and After* ("Dylan Thomas: A Pioneer"), was one of the very few critics who paused long enough to examine the sonnets for technique and meaning. He combined a general summary with a concrete interpretation to offer the reader one of the earliest and most perceptive

guides to an understanding of the poem. Mr. Scarfe
noticed the unity of the sonnets at once:

These so-called "sonnets" (they are 14-line poems)
cannot be considered separately, as together they
form a unit . . . The technique is cumulative, im-
pressionistic, though in one or two sonnets the
subject is directly presented. Subjects, rather, for
though the theme is the life-death antagonism, it
is inextricably bound up with Old and New Testa-
ment mythology and sexual symbolism.[10]

However, to Marshall Stearns the sonnets did not ap-
pear as a unit. In an essay called "Unsex the Skeleton:
Notes on the Poetry of Dylan Thomas" in *Sewanee Re-
view*, Volume LII (Summer, 1944), Mr. Stearns singled
out the eighth sonnet as the "climax in a series of ten
loosely connected sonnets." He believed that the eighth
sonnet could "be treated independently without loss of
meaning" and offered an interpretation which centers
on the role of Mary:

The lines may best be explained . . . as the poet's
attempt to describe the crucifixion as interpreted
by Mary, the mother of God, the mother of Jesus,
and the source of all creation. The key to the poem
is the fundamental contrast between the earthly
and the heavenly Mary. . . . At the most crucial
moment of all time, when man becomes god and
mortality immortality, she plays the one essential
role and through her, sex rises to asexual and eter-
nal glory.

Francis Scarfe and Marshall Stearns differ only in their
view of the structure of the poem; essentially their in-
terpretations of the poem are similar: a sexual theme
conveyed in Biblical imagery.

David Daiches considered the sonnets dense and con-
gested:

The sonnet-sequence . . . contains some brilliant
identifying imagery (suggesting the identity of
man with Christ, of creation with death, of history

with the present), but it is altogether too closely packed, too dense, to come across effectively. The opening is almost a self-parody . . . The careful explicator will be able to produce informative glosses on each of these phrases, but the fact remains that the poem is congested with metaphors; and the reader is left with a feeling of oppression.[11]

Elder Olson, in his sensitive appraisal of Dylan Thomas's work, *The Poetry of Dylan Thomas,* devoted a lengthy chapter to the sonnets. Professor Olson regarded the sonnets as a single poem and believed the sequence to be the most difficult of Thomas's poems:

> . . . Like many other poems of Thomas, they are difficult in their diction, and present other difficulties as well; but their special problems stem from the complexity, rather than the mere fact, of their symbolism.[12]

Professor Olson believed that this complex symbolism "involves at least six distinguishable levels, which the poet intricately interrelates." Of the six levels which he mentions, Professor Olson chooses the last three levels for his exegesis of the sonnets: the Hercules myth, the constellations, and a Christian interpretation derived from the myth of Hercules and the constellation Hercules.

William York Tindall, in his comprehensive, stimulating study, *A Reader's Guide to Dylan Thomas,* believed

> . . . that the theme [of the sonnets] is Thomas himself, the constant subject of his verse and prose. Although cheerfully allowing the presence of Jesus, Hercules, the stars, zodiac, and a generally neglected voyage, I think them analogies, not to be confused with theme.[13]

I believe the sonnets are a deeply moving statement of religious perplexity concluding in spiritual certainty. They reflect the wonder, awe, doubt, and faith of a young poet who could not reconcile the capacity of divine pity with the necessity of human sacrifice. The paradox of the Incarnation and Passion affected Dylan Thomas early in his career. He was twenty-one years old when he wrote these sonnets, the same age at which Milton wrote "On the Morning of Christ's Nativity." "We were both religious poets," wrote Vernon Watkins about Thomas and himself.[14] There is a revelation in the sonnets of a fearful struggle of the poet with his God. Concentric to the theme of struggle is the theme of sacrifice: the agonizing story of Abraham and Isaac is implicit in the sonnets. Mount Moriah and Calvary loom large in this poem.

The first seven sonnets are earthbound, as if the Word were imprisoned in clay. It is in the eighth sonnet that Thomas's doubt wrestles with faith as he sees in the Crucifixion the triumph of eternity over pain. The ninth sonnet wavers between weariness and expectancy. In the tenth sonnet Thomas's soul is brushed by an angel's wing, and in the last lines of the poem prophecy and credo ring plangently of the green garden and the everlasting mercy. The poem begins with a sonnet mocking the descent of the Word; it concludes in a spiraling ascent of faith.

1

Sonnet I

And the Word was made flesh
John 1:14

'Twas much, that man was made like God before,
But, that God should be made like man, much more.
John Donne, Sonnet XV, *Holy Sonnets*

THE RELIGIOUS SONNETS are a sequence of ten units of
fourteen lines each, arranged in sestet and octave.
Through half-rhymes, so effectively used by Wilfred
Owen, Thomas achieved a rugged, harsh, uneven sound
consistent with the theme of his poem. A neat rhyme
scheme would not have suggested the upheaval of chaos
in Genesis nor the agony of the Passion and Crucifixion.

The pattern of the poem is similar to the sequence of
medieval pageant plays, each sonnet a tableau, moving
from the Incarnation through the Crucifixion to an
apocalyptic prophecy. Here, as in a pageant play, in-
nocence and religiosity, awe and familiarity, devotion
and ribaldry are curiously mixed.

The themes of this poem recall several seventeenth-
century sequences of religious poetry as well as the
sermons of Lancelot Andrewes on the Nativity, Pas-
sion, and Resurrection. Robert Herrick's *Noble Numbers*
is an example of such a sequence, where, as Herrick
himself tells us in the subtitle, "he sings the Birth of
his Christ: and sighes for his Saviours suffering on the

Crosse." Richard Crashaw's *Carmen Deo Nostro*, especially the "Sancta Maria" and "Upon the Bleeding Crucifix," offers an interesting comparison to Thomas's baroque imagery, particularly in the eighth sonnet. In George Herbert's "The Sacrifice" (from *The Temple*) the reader may find an opportunity to compare the use of the first person singular, in Christ's own account of the Passion, with Thomas's ambiguous use of "I" in the sequence. John Donne's *Divine Poems* serve as an excellent paradigm for the ten sonnets, especially the "La Corona" sequence, the second group of "Holy Sonnets," "The Crosse," "Resurrection, imperfect," "The Annunciation and Passion," and parts of "The Litanie." Milton's *Paradise Lost* in its panoramic treatment of the Christian drama from the account of Satanic disobedience to the Vision of the Last Trump is an incomparable complement to Thomas's poem. Milton's spectacle of the Creation out of "Chaos and Old Night" is on the same heroic scale as Michelangelo's ceiling in the Sistine Chapel; Thomas's account of the Creation is more like a surrealist wasteland of Dali. Milton describes the grand majesty of the Father accepting the infinite pity of the Son; Thomas shows us an implacable Father demanding an inexorable sacrifice of the Son.

The first sonnet is a transformation of the Nativity story according to St. Luke. This is no traditional treatment of the Christmas theme. The pastoral setting of shepherds and their flocks, the blaze of light which enveloped them as they heard the tidings of the Nativity, the angelic host which praised God belong to an annunciation of joy and hope. Neither joy nor hope is evident in Thomas's version. The sonnet is charged with mystery, suspense, and imminent disaster. The atmosphere suggests the kind of treatment De Chirico would have given the Nativity had he painted it: a mysterious, shadowy infinity in which lurked latent horror about to be born, as the fleshless Word descends scrapingly toward Bethlehem.

The sequence begins with "altarwise," suggesting not only a ritual offering but also the position of a sacrificial victim as he "lay graveward." [1] "Owl-light" is dusk, the eerie half-light which distorts shape, blurs outlines, and suggests an expectancy of a mysterious event about to happen.[2] The identity of the gentleman "in the half-way house" is unknown to us. Is he God about to descend to mortality ("graveward")? Or is the gentleman Abaddon? Or is he Christ? He is all three in one: he is God, he is Christ, he is Abaddon. Although Thomas's religious themes are in the orthodox tradition of Christianity, his imagery is not restricted by theology. It is possible for him to conceive of an image of the Trinity such as God–Christ–Abaddon, suggesting divinity, humanity, and mortality at once. The retinue of furies is hardly the multitude of the heavenly host described in Luke. Why Thomas chose Greek mythological agents as an escort for Abaddon it is difficult to understand, since they seem to be more appropriate to a fallen angel than to the descended Word. I believe that the furies are Thomas's transformation of those horrendous locusts of Abaddon, with scorpion's stings, faces of men, hair of women, and teeth of lions described in Revelation 9: 7–8. Thomas makes a concentrated effort to transmute all the hope, light, and wonder in St. Luke's Nativity into bleakness, darkness, and horror. Furies, instead of angels, are at home in this sonnet. Since they are chthonic daughters of night, what more fearfully appropriate retinue than they? The "half-way house" in which the gentleman lodger is accommodated is not the inn which St. Luke tells us was crowded. It may be the indefinite point in infinity where the descending Word is poised halfway between Heaven and earth; or it may be the manger in which Christ is born; or it may possibly be the Incarnation itself, which was Christ's halfway house between eternity and Resurrection. It may even be Mary's womb, which Donne described as "a place of middle kind." [3]

14

Abaddon is the Angel of the Bottomless Pit (described also as Apollyon) in Revelation 9:11, where his function is different from the one ascribed to him by Thomas. The Hebrew meaning of the name Abaddon is literally "place of perishing." It occurs in the Old Testament (in Hebrew) at least five times: Job 26:6, 31:12; Psalms 88:12; and Proverbs 15:11, 27:20. Thomas personified the "place of perishing," as St. John did; but to Thomas Abaddon is the Angel of Death. There is a similar personification in the Apocrypha of the New Testament. Bartholomew the Apostle, in the Book of the Resurrection of Christ, describes the bewilderment of Death as he comes to the tomb of Christ and finds it empty:

> Now Death came into the tomb of the Saviour, and he found it lighted up with the light of life, and he went into the back of the tomb, and seated himself there with his ministers. Now Abbatôn, who is Death, and Gaios, and Tryphon, and Ophiath, and Phthinon, and Sotormis, and Komphion, who are the six sons of Death, wriggled into the tomb of the Son of God on their faces in the form of serpents (?), wriggling in with their great thief in very troth. These robbers and evil-doers were lying in wait for the moment the Saviour would go down into the Amente [the nether world], so that they might enter with him, and know what it was that he would do.[4]

I do not know whether Thomas had ever looked at this portion of the Apocrypha, but I offer a parallel in imagery and personification as an astonishing instance of similarity between two works as remote from each other as Thomas's sonnets are from St. Bartholomew's account of the Resurrection. Not only does Abaddon appear in the Apocrypha as Death, but he also comes with a retinue of six assistants. Are these the counterparts of Thomas's "furies" who are the escort of the gentleman in the half-way house?

15

The presence of Abaddon "in the hang-nail cracked from Adam" reminds us of mortality brought into the world through Adam's sin. But Abaddon is not the only descendant of Adam; Christ, too, in the flesh, is kin to Adam. (In Luke 3:23–38 Christ's genealogy is traced to Adam.) The hangnail image is a typical Thomas pun: a hangnail, literally, is a cracked piece of skin hanging from the finger. As a metaphor, "hangnail" contains genealogy and prophecy: it is a statement that Christ (the cuticle) is descended from Adam (the finger), and it is a prediction that Christ will hang nailed to the Cross.

The feeling of dread is heightened by all the connotations of death suggested in the legend of the mandrake and the vocabulary of sensational journalism. No good tidings are brought this night by an angel of the Lord; instead, the baleful scream of a mandrake heralds the birth of Christ. Thomas's use of the mandrake legend is a striking example of the multiple meanings his imagery can be made to yield. The mandrake has a bifurcated root, giving the appearance of a tiny human form. It was rare, valuable, and dangerous to obtain. Medieval legend endowed it with the power to induce fecundity and assuage pain.[5] In order to uproot a mandrake one had to avoid being within hearing distance of its fatal scream; therefore, a dog was tied to a mandrake root and lured forward with the promise of a bit of food held at a safe distance from the mandrake. The dog lurched forward to grab the food, pulling the mandrake out of the earth; and at that moment the piercing, deadly scream of the mandrake killed the dog. Thomas made only a few minor changes in the legend: the bifurcated root becomes Abaddon's fork (loins); the mandrake's scream is "tomorrow's scream"; and the dog bites out (rather than pulls out) the root. By having the dog bite out the mandrake, Thomas shifts the emphasis from the mandrake to the dog: dog biting mandrake is word-

16

MANDRAKE AND DOG
From a manuscript of the thirteenth century
in the British Museum

play on the news value of man bites dog, a part of the involved journalistic image in the three lines.

The journalistic metaphor consists of the dog, "jaw for news," "tomorrow's scream," and "atlas-eater." Since an important event is about to take place, Thomas treats the imminent Nativity, with its implied Crucifixion, as if it were a screaming headline, proclaiming the event to newspaper readers who wake up to find the world transformed on that first Christmas day. "The atlas-eater with a jaw for news" is newspaper vocabulary. The dog is regarded as a keen-scented reporter on the trail of an important story. "Jaw" is slang for talk, but it is also a reworking of "nose for news." The sense of the image is that of a reporter devouring a sensational story for world-wide distribution, "atlas-eater" suggesting the annihilation of distance. "Atlas" is also a technical term in the vocabulary of paper producers; it is a specific size of paper sheet, known in England as a "small atlas" (25 inches x 31 inches). Perhaps Thomas was suggesting the vast amounts of paper that would have been consumed in printing the account of the Nativity, had there been newspapers in the ancient world. The "fairies" among whom the dog bites out the mandrake are puzzling creatures. Are they the sexless angels of Abaddon's retinue? Are they the creatures abroad this magic night who are charged with announcing an important event? Are they in opposition to the furies? Are they the furies transformed into a half-rhyme by the poet as conjurer? Perhaps the furies and fairies are an echo of Marcellus' description of the time of Christ's Nativity, when

> The nights are wholesome, then no planets strike,
> No fairy takes, nor witch hath power to charm,
> So hallowed, and so gracious is that time.
>   (*Hamlet*, I, 1, 164–165)

In the rapid action of the sonnet the images shift in

18

meaning. Thomas may have overdeveloped a journalistic metaphor ("tomorrow's scream") at the same time that he was offering a bold theological metaphor. The dog may be Christ, the hound of Heaven, who bites out the mandrake (man) from the fork or loins of Abaddon, thus redeeming man from sin (Adam) and death (Abaddon). "Tomorrow's scream" foretells the Crucifixion at the same time that it suggests screaming headlines of the event. The scream also reminds us that Christ, like the dog, must die to uproot man from his fallen condition. The patristic commentaries on the Song of Solomon (7:13) suggest that "the dead who were raised with Christ were mandrakes, for the mandrake has a human form, and stands for dead men." [6] One can see the possibility of a similar meaning in the dog and mandrake image: that of mankind awaiting liberation from death (Abaddon) by Christ.

The source of Thomas's mandrake image must remain a matter of conjecture. There are many references to the mandrake in Shakespeare and Donne.[7] Two other sources may be J. R. Harris's "Origin of the Cult of Aphrodite" and C. J. S. Thompson's *The Mystic Mandrake;* the latter work was published in London a year before Thomas's sonnets appeared in print in December, 1935. The dates may be coincidental, but a poet who fashioned the mandrake legend into an image several times in his poetry and prose, within a period of a few years, must have discovered more about it than he could have found in seventeenth-century literature.[8] The reproduction on page 17 and the two quotations below may give the reader a possible source of Thomas's imagery.

J. R. Harris quoted ancient authorities in his description of uprooting a mandrake:

. . . the mandrake is a root which shrieks terribly when you pull it out of the ground; it is, indeed, so dangerous that you must not try to pull it: better tie a dog to the stalk and then entice the dog to-

wards you with a *bonne bouche:* stop your ears by
way of precaution, and use your eyes to see the
last dying agonies of the dog who has pulled the
root for you. Then go and pick it up. To your sur-
prise, you will find the root to have a human form,
sometimes male, and sometimes female . . .[9]

C. J. S. Thompson repeats much of what Harris says
but adds the following bit of lore:

In some parts of Wales the mandrake superstitions
were also connected with briony with its dark
green leaves and red berries . . . Its leaves and
fruit were called "charnel food" and it was believed
only to grow beside the gallows tree . . . Fur-
thermore, when uprooted it was said to utter shrieks
and groans like a human being, and its agony was
dreadful to hear . . . In other districts of Wales
there was a belief in the legend that the mandrake
grew from the tears of an innocent man who had
been hanged on the gallows.[10]

The octave introduces a conventional figure of Death,
bare-boned and penny-eyed. At the sound of the man-
drake's scream the gentleman who "lay graveward"
rises to a vertical posture and becomes the "walking
word," moving "Christward" to identify himself to the
child in the cradle. A reference to the old burial cus-
tom of placing pennies on the eyelids of the dead height-
ens the horror of this image of walking death.[11] Abad-
don now undergoes a startling transformation. A few
lines above we learned of his ancestry: he is the ragged
cuticle of Adam, death born of sin. We also learned
that he was a mysterious traveler, a lodger in a halfway
house, having arrived at dusk. As he leaves the half-
way house, now a "gentleman of wounds," we do not
know whether he is the wounded, the wounder, or
both. He may be wounded because of the radical muti-
lation by the dog among the fairies. He may be the
wounder implying or forecasting the Crucifixion. An-
other transformation reveals the gentleman as an ob-

scene old skeleton ("bones unbuttoned") and an "old cock from nowheres and the heaven's egg," a celestial hobo with a vague genealogy, "hatched from the windy salvage on one leg." "Windy salvage" is a double pun: it may refer to the heavenly junkyard whence this derelict comes; or it may be a reference to the divine breath, the Word that saves.

The descent of the Holy Spirit is symbolized, in Scripture and in art, by a dove winging downward in a radiant stream of light. Thomas transforms the dove into a Disney-like, molted old cock. There it stands on one leg, scraping at the cradle on Christmas Eve, announcing its identity. The image is drawn from a legend about a cock which began crowing "Christus natus est" at the moment of the Nativity.[12]

The rest of the sonnet seems to merge a scene of a medieval crèche with a *danse macabre*. "Old cock from nowheres" is in metaphorical apposition to the "gentleman of wounds," who is Abaddon. We learn, too, that he comes from the Heaven's egg, a reference to one of many autogenetic myths of God creating himself out of an egg.[13] There is a fascinating parallel to Thomas's "hatched from the windy salvage" in a choral ode of cosmogony from *The Birds* of Aristophanes:

> At first there was Chaos, and Erebos, and Night
> . . . until, at last, in the deep dark bosom of Erebos an egg, wind-begotten, was laid by black-winged Night.
> And from that egg . . . sprang Eros . . .
> Mating with dark Chaos, Eros hatched us . . .[14]

The slang epithet "old cock" suggests the ancient of days, the old chief or boss; at the same time it is an obsolete corruption of God's name in oaths. Since the cock is a symbol of virility, "old cock from nowheres" is a pun, in street language, implying the inexplicable conception of Christ.[15] In the description of the fleshless Word descending like an obscene old hobo "with bones unbuttoned," Thomas once more merges Abaddon with

God. Completing his trinity, he moved this skeletal avatar from a windy eternity into "that night of time" to announce itself to the Child in the manger:

> I am the long world's gentleman, he said,
> And share my bed with Capricorn and Cancer.

In this annunciation, so unlike Gabriel's, the gentleman identifies himself not only with the sun but with all the slain and resurrected gods. "Long world's gentleman" suggests an elongated, angular, tortured El Greco figure stretched longitudinally over an elliptoid globe from the northern tropic (Cancer) to the southern (Capricorn). In this image we have a composite metaphor of sacrificed gods: Osiris, Adonis, Tammuz, Attis, and now Christ. These are solar gods who share their beds with Capricorn and Cancer; they are buried in darkness and rise in light. Sir Thomas Browne describes, in the same zodiacal language, the progress of the soul which "came down by Cancer, and ascended by Capricornus." [16]

The zodiacal signs are always used metaphorically by Thomas. In the last line they foretell the career of Christ, who is born in December, near enough to the twenty-first of the month to place him in Capricorn, which is the tenth sign beginning at the most southerly point of the ecliptic or winter solstitial point. The fourth sign of the zodiac (Cancer), beginning at the most northerly point of the ecliptic or summer solstitial point, the twenty-first of June, signifies that the sun-god is at his highest pitch of glory and is coming to his doom.[17] On this note the first sonnet ends. There is no angelic doxology sung, there are no astonished exclamations of the shepherds. The only sounds we hear are tomorrow's scream, the wind, and the scraping at the cradle. The rest is dark silence.

2

Sonnet II

. . there shall come a Star out of Jacob, and a sceptre
shall rise out of Israel . . .

Numbers 24:17

To make a child, now swadled, to proceede Man, and then
shoote up . . .

Ben Jonson, Prologue to
Everyman in His Humour

THE SECOND SONNET continues the paradox of the Na-
tivity: the child nursed at its mother's breast is the man
who will drink hyssop on the Cross. To Thomas the
epiphany of hope is only another metaphor of death,
another shape or apparition in one history. The sonnet
recalls a sixteenth-century carol and Milton's "On the
Morning of Christ's Nativity":

Jesu, God's Son, born He was
In a crib with hay and grass,
And died for us on the Cross
Gloria Tibi, Domine.[1]

The Babe lies yet in smiling Infancy,
That on the bitter cross
Must redeem our loss

(Stanza xvi, ll. 151–153)

There is a distortion of traditional Nativity episodes:
the Child suckled at his mother's breast in the manger
becomes "the child that sucketh long"; the star of Beth-

lehem which guided the Magi is changed to a long
stick set alight from the cradle; the joyous angels are
wrenched from the familiar attitude of adoration and
are transformed from beatific creatures into a "hollow
agent."

The galactic pelican image is an instance of Thomas's
ability to "stride on two levels." [2] He can suggest, in
this metaphor, the picture of the infant Jesus being
suckled at his mother's breast; and simultaneously he
can leap thirty-three years forward toward the long
wound of the Crucifixion implied in the pelican image.
"The child that sucketh long is shooting up," is Biblical
in tone in its deliberate use of the old third person singu-
lar ending; and it is an echo of Ben Jonson's "To make
a child, now swadled, to proceede / Man, and then
shoote up . . ." from *Every Man In His Humour* (Pro-
logue, I, 7–9). Pun, metaphor, and bestiary legend are
fused in "Planet-ducted pelican of circles." Packed into
this line is a varied vocabulary: astronomical ("planet"),
anatomical ("ducted"), ornithological ("pelican"), geo-
metrical ("circles"); and a rather involved pun:
planet-ducted = galaxy = milky way = breast (circles)
A similar pun appears in an earlier poem of Thomas's:

The mouth of time sucked, like a sponge,

The milky acid on each hinge,

And swallowed dry the waters of the breast.

When the galactic sea was sucked . . . [3]

The pelican image is a little more familiar than
"planet-ducted," since it is in the tradition of Christian
art, where the pelican is a symbol of charity, of Christ's
sacrifice, redemption, and resurrection. The legend of
the pelican feeding her young with her own blood by
piercing her breast with her bill is found in the medieval
bestiary.[4] In heraldry the representation is described as
"a pelican in her piety," the word "piety" having the
classical meaning of filial devotion. The heraldic em-
blem depicting the pelican standing over her nest, wings
extended, pricking her breast from which drops of blood

fall, gives us the term "pelican vulning herself." In the hymn, "Adoro te devote," ascribed to St. Thomas Aquinas, Christ is addressed as the "tender pelican":

Pie pellicane, Jesu Domine
Me immundum munda tuo sanguine:
Cuius una stilla salvum facere
Totum mundum quit ab omni scelere.

[Oh tender pelican, Jesus Lord,
Purify me, who am unclean, in your blood,
One drop of which can save
The whole world from all its sin.] [5]

And Dante, describing John, the beloved disciple, leaning on Christ's breast, has Beatrice say (in the Heaven of Fixed Stars, *Paradiso*, Canto XXV, l. 113):

Questi è colui che giacque sopra'l petto del
nostro pellicano,

[This is he who leaned upon the breast of our
Pelican,]

Perhaps it was among the Elizabethan poets that Thomas discovered pelican lore. Dekker, for example, in his *Four Birds in Noah's Arke* uses the image as Thomas does:

The nature of the Pellican is to peck her owne bosom, and with the drops of her blood to feede her yong ones.[6]

Shakespeare uses the image in at least three plays: *Richard II, King Lear,* and *Hamlet.*[7]

The nursing image is continued in the third line ("Weans on an artery the gender's strip") in a departure from legend and literature into slang and pun. "The gender's strip" is Thomas's slang for male genitals. The child is weaned on the artery of its own mother; and it is blood, not milk, that he drinks, that very blood which he will later shed on the Cross. There is a similar theme in a dialogue between Mary and Christ, in a fifteenth-century carol, in which the flow of milk and

25

blood is described as a contrast between the security of the child in his mother's arms and his agony on the Cross:

> As she Him held [all] in her lap,
> He took her lovely by the pap,
> And then sweetly He took a nap
> And sucked his fill of the liquor.
>
> To His mother gan He say:
> "For this milk one muste die,
> It is my kind therewith to play
> My sweet mother, *par amour.*"
>
> The maiden freely gan to sing
> And in her song she made mourning,
> How He that is our heavenly King
> Should shed His blood with great dolour.[8]

Thomas's lines also recall Gerard Manley Hopkins's beautifully moving stanza from *The Wreck of the Deutschland,* in which he compresses the themes described above:

> It dates from day
> Of his going in Galilee;
> Warm-laid grave of a womb-life grey;
> Manger, maiden's knee;
> The dense and the driven Passion, and fright-
> sweat; [9]

The theme of conception, growth, and development is repeated in Thomas's imagery of ignition:

> Child of the short spark in a shapeless country
> Soon sets alight a long stick from the cradle;

"The short spark in a shapeless country" is Thomas's metaphor of the inexplicable conception in electrical terms: generation, dynamic energy, and spark gap. The "shapeless country" is from Thomas's own atlas of metaphors: it is Mary's womb, a frequent image in his poems, since gestation to him is always a journey and the womb is always a shapeless country.[10] There is a

26

possibility that the "shapeless country" is an extension, in more concrete language, of the womb image of the first sonnet in which "nowheres," "the heaven's egg," and "windy salvage" describe a celestial womb in which God begets himself. Here, however, "nowheres" and "windy salvage" become the "shapeless country," the physical womb in which the second begetting, the Incarnation, takes place. There is a third possibility. The shapeless country may be amorphous geography, but "shape in one history" suggests form, outline, and finiteness: the Word taking fetal shape as it becomes flesh in time.

The imagery of ignition is carried into the next line. The short spark blazons a sign in the sky. The "long stick" which is set alight is the Cross, seen now as the beam of light radiating from the manger crib into the sky. The "long stick" together with Jacob and the stars is a phallic pun and an astronomical metaphor. A Jacob's staff (from Jacobus, the Apostle James, not Jacob of the Old Testament) is a pilgrim's staff, or a cross-staff. It is also the name given an obsolete instrument used in measuring heights and distances in navigation. The child in the "shapeless country" sets alight the long stick enabling the Magi to take their bearings.[11] The short spark is now the brilliant star over Bethlehem. An excerpt from the Protevangelion (15:19) in the New Testament Apocrypha illuminates this passage:

. . . the star which they [the Wise Men] saw in the east went before them, till it came and stood over the cave where the young child was with Mary his mother.

The next four lines of the sonnet are developed through a use of Biblical, nautical, and piratical imagery:

The horizontal cross-bones of Abaddon
You by the cavern over the black stairs,
Rung bone and blade, the verticals of Adam,[12]
And, manned by midnight, Jacob to the stars.

The "horizontal cross-bones of Abaddon" image serves four purposes:

1. It reintroduces Abaddon and Adam (of whom Christ is created) and links them with Jacob.

2. It is an elliptical image of skull and crossbones, a familiar symbol of warning on poison labels, danger signs, and pirates' flags.

3. It introduces, through its piratical image, the nautical image of a Jacob's ladder (with its vocabulary of "rung" and "manned") which in turn suggests a Biblical reference to Jacob's dream.

4. It foreshadows the Cross, which is made of a crosspiece and a shaft (the horizontals of Abaddon, the verticals of Adam); or metaphorically stated, it is the Cross which grew out of sin (Adam) and death (Abaddon).

The difficulties of syntax in lines 7–10 leave one a little bewildered. However, if the lines are rearranged in a syntactical paraphrase, they gain in clarity: "You, by the cavern over the black stairs, who rung bone and blade, the horizontal cross-bones of Abaddon to the verticals of Adam, you are the same one who hoisted [rung] Jacob to the stars." In the vocative "You by the cavern over the black stairs," Thomas calls to God accusingly, tauntingly. The line suggests a conspiracy plotted by a political boss and his henchmen (God and his angels) in a dim room over the back stairs. There is an ironic quality in this image of contrast between two promises. At Bethel, as Jacob dreamed in the night of angels ascending and descending a ladder, God appeared to him and promised him a bright future. That promise was fulfilled.[13] But on this "night of time" at Bethlehem, God marks a sign in the sky over the cave of the Nativity as a promise of hope, and then fashions out of the bones of Adam and Abaddon his doublecross on which Christ is nailed.

The ladder image, based on Bible and legend, becomes a pun. Literally, the ladder refers to Jacob's dream, but it also implies the Incarnation of the Word as it descended the ladder of bones wrought of Abaddon and Adam. And, finally, it is the ladder from the legends of the Crucifixion, by means of which Christ is removed from the Cross. "Rung" evolves from the ladder of bones image; as a verb it takes three objects ("bone," "blade," and "Jacob") and has two possible meanings: it may mean joined or girt (as in "You, God, joined bone and blade and fashioned man"); or it may mean to reach by a ladder, a reference to Jacob who was "rung to the stars," or raised to eminence by God's favor.

"Manned by midnight" suggests a crew of angels manning the ladder at midnight. The word "manned" is consistent with the nautical term of Jacob's ladder and the piratical image of crossed bones. The cavern may be the midnight sky in Jacob's dream, the Nativity cave, or the cave donated by Joseph of Arimathea for Christ's burial. The possibility of the cavern's being both birthplace and burial place is not remote, particularly when we remember that the sonnet begins with "Death is all metaphors" and then develops into an image of gestation in the sestet, followed by an image of death in the octave. Crashaw, in his miniature poem, "To Our Blessed Lord Upon the Choice of His Sepulchre," combines the birth and death of Christ in a tight conceit on almost the same theme:

> How life and death in Thee
> > Agree!
> Thou hadst a virgin womb,
> > And tomb.
> A Joseph did betroth
> > Them both.[14]

We have had the first warning: God who can raise Jacob to the stars can nail Jesus to the Cross. The warning is repeated by the hollow agent:

> Hairs of your head, then said the hollow agent,

> Are but the roots of nettles and of feathers

This is an ironic reference to the parable of the sparrows and the numbered hairs of the head (Matthew 10:29–31). The warning is a taunting reminder of God's doublecross, a grievance which Thomas held in an earlier poem ("Before I Knocked"):

> Remember me and pity Him
> Who took my flesh and bone for armour
> And doublecrossed my mother's womb.[15]

In the parable we are assured that nothing escapes God's notice; not even a sparrow worth half a farthing falls to the ground:

> Are not two sparrows sold for a farthing? and one of them shall not fall on the ground without your Father. But the hairs of your head are all numbered. Fear ye not therefore, ye are of more value than many sparrows.
>
> (Matthew 10:29)

Recalling this assurance, Thomas reminds us that Christ's is one head, however, that will not be protected. The hairs of this head are numbered, and the head is destined for a crown of nettles. The birth and growth of Christ and the growth of the tree on which he will be crucified are described in parallel imagery. There is a suggestion of inevitability here: the push of the child's head through the womb is as inexorable as the relentless pressure of the tree's roots "through a pavement." Christ, in the fullness of his manhood, will wear the nettles; the rood tree, in the fullness of its bloom, will be cut down.

According to one legend of the rood the wood of the Cross was made of palm, cypress, cedar, and olive.[16] Thomas, however, creates his own legend of the rood and describes the cross tree as a hemlock. The description is neither arbitrary nor incongruous, for in the epithet "hemlock-headed" there are several associations suggested: Christ's prayer in Gethsemane (Mark 14:36), "take away this cup from me," with its elliptical reference to wormwood and gall; the hyssop which Christ drank on the Cross; and lastly the hemlock of another execution in antiquity, that of Socrates.[17] "Hemlock-headed" led me to the interesting discovery that the word for "hemlock" and "head" in Hebrew is *rosh*. I do not suggest this as evidence of Thomas's knowledge of Hebrew; however, he may have been aware of the references to hemlock in the Old Testament. It is mentioned at least three times: in Deuteronomy 29:18, Hosea 10:4, and Amos 6:12; and in the first two instances the word *rosh* appears in the margin of cross-references and notes in the Authorized and Revised versions.[18]

The image of a nestling bird is developed through "feathers over these groundworks." Christ the fledgling will leave his mother as inevitably as birds take wing. And as inevitably as the sparrow falls to earth, so will Christ fall under the weight of his Cross. Death as a feather is an image that occurs at least four times in three poems.[19] The "wood of weathers" recalls Lancelot Andrewes's description of Christ, betrayed and deserted: ". . . and He [was] left in the state of a weather-beaten tree, all desolate and forlorn."[20]

The last four lines of the sonnet are an ironic paraphrase of the parable of the sparrows and a modified version of Isaiah 53:2, 3:

> For he shall grow up before him as a tender plant, and as a root of a dry ground ["roots . . . over these groundworks"]: he hath no form nor comeliness; and when we shall see him, there is no beauty that we should desire him. He is despised and rejected of men; a man of sorrows, and acquainted with grief.

It is in Isaiah (11:1), too, that we find the prophecy:

> And there shall come forth a rod out of the stem of Jesse, and a branch shall grow out of his roots.

The tree of Jesse took root in Bethlehem, grew in Nazareth, and was cut down in Jerusalem.

3

Sonnet III

O strong Ramme, which hast batter'd heaven for mee,
Mild Lambe, which with thy blood, has marked the
    path; . . .

         John Donne, "Ascension," *Holy Sonnets*

For before the Nativity is the dead of the winter and after
    it the quick.

         Christopher Smart, *Jubilate Agno*, XI

THE THIRD SONNET is woven of images from Genesis, the
Gospels, the Incarnation, medieval legends of Adam,
puns, the zodiac, Shakespeare, Milton, Washington Irv-
ing, and one of Thomas's unpublished poems. There are
three distinct parts in the third sonnet: the Atonement
of Christ for Adam's sin ("Adam's wether"), the In-
carnation ("descended bone"), and a zodiacal metaphor
of seasons ("black ram"). The imagery falls into five
categories, giving the sonnet an order which neither
anarchic syntax nor disjointed chronology can disrupt:

sheep	*seasons*	*Bible*
lamb	three dead seasons	Adam
wether	shuffling of the year	Eve
flock of	old winter	tree-tailed worm
horns	weathering changes	skullfoot
butt	twice spring	[Golgotha]
horned	chimed	garden time [Eden]
down		thunderous pave-
black ram		ments

sheep	*Bible*
mutton fold	the descended bone
	[Incarnation]

sex	*death*
worm that mounted Eve	climbing grave
marrow-laddle	skullfoot
descended bone	vaults
mutton fold	undertaker's van

Springtime is the season in this sonnet, but there are no gamboling lambs; instead, there is a lamb on knocking knees. The lamb is the traditional paschal offering, later becoming, among the Israelites, a zodiacal sign for the first month of the year (Nisan or March–April). When John the Baptist pointed to Jesus, saying "Behold the Lamb of God," he was referring to the description of the paschal offering in Exodus 12:5, "Your lamb shall be without blemish, a male of the first year." Among the Christians the lamb became the Eucharistic victim— perfect, holy, and unblemished.

The first line of the sonnet is salvaged from one of Thomas's unpublished poems (MS, May 13, 1933).[1] The seven lines quoted below indicate the origin of the ovine imagery in the third sonnet (line numbers of the MS poem are indicated in parentheses):

First there was the lamb on knocking knees, (1)

First there was the lamb which grew a sheep. (6)

First there was the spring lamb which grew bigger; (11)

The lamb grown sheep had lambs around its belly (22)

And teats like turnips for the lambs to bully; (23)

The black sheep, shuffling of the fold, old winter; (33)

There's nothing but the lamb on knocking knees; (37)

33

The "three dead seasons" may be a hyperbolic description of the three days marking the time between Good Friday and Easter Sunday when hope was as lifeless as the body of Christ sealed in the tomb. Or perhaps the dead seasons for Thomas are what they are for Lancelot Andrewes, who sees in the coincidence of the Passover with the rebirth of spring "the renewing sweet time":

> And even nature's Passover, the general Passover is even at this time, both in Heaven and earth. Above in Heaven, where the sun having past over all the signs is come about, and renews his course at the first sign in the Zodiac. And beneath in earth, from the sharp time of winter, and fermenting time of the earth, to the renewing sweet time; the time of the spring, wherein there is *nova conspersio* [a new sprinkling] in nature itself. And why should not the Passover of grace be now likewise in season, and have due concurrence with nature? [2]

The "climbing grave" is also a possible reference to the Cross which, according to legend, grew as a tree out of Adam's grave. The origin of the legend can be found in the Book of Enoch in the Pseudepigrapha of the Old Testament. Medieval sources of the legend are the *Legenda Aurea* and the *Travels of Sir John Mandeville*.[3] The most familiar reference to this legend is in Donne's "Hymn to God my God, in my sickness":

> We thinke that Paradise and Calvarie,
> Christs Crosse, and Adams tree, stood in one
>   place;

In a synthesis of the legend, S. Baring-Gould in his *Curious Myths of the Middle Ages* tells the story of Seth's journey to the barred gates of Paradise, where a cherub on guard informs Seth that "the wood whereon redemption shall be won shall grow from the tomb of thy father." Seth is then shown a tree, the root of which grows down to Hell and the summit of which reaches Heaven. The cherub takes three seeds from the tree and

34

gives them to Seth with instructions to place them in Adam's mouth upon his father's death. Three days after Seth's return Adam dies, and Seth carries out the cherub's instructions. Baring-Gould's account of the legend continues:

> Then his son buried him . . . and his sepulchre was on Golgotha. In course of time three trees grew from the seeds brought from Paradise: one was a cedar, another a cypress, and a third, a pine. They grew with prodigious force, thrusting their boughs to right and left . . . After a while three trees touched one another, then began to incorporate and confound their several natures in a single trunk.[4]

The legend is mentioned by Jung, who repeated Baring-Gould's version and added to it a soterial theme:

> The student of medieval history is familiar with the representation of the cross growing above the grave of Adam. The legend was that Adam was buried on Golgotha. Seth had planted on his grave a branch of the "paradise tree," which became the cross and tree of death of Christ. We all know that through Adam's guilt, sin and death came into the world, and Christ through his death has redeemed us from the guilt.[5]

"Flock of horns" extends the ovine imagery. It is a synecdoche which, in the language of the Apocrypha, stands for Adam's progeny, among whom the wether is bruised and crushed. The language in the Book of Enoch offers an interesting parallel to Thomas's imagery. The first quotation describes the ram beset by enemies; the second describes, in the metaphor of the horned lamb, the Messianic leader:

> And that ram began to butt on either side those dogs, foxes, and wild boars till he had destroyed them all.
>
> (89:42)
>
> . . . and the first among them became a lamb, and

35

that lamb a great animal and had great black horns
on its head.

(90:38)

In the line "Butt of the tree-tailed worm that
mounted Eve," we have an echo of *Paradise Lost.* The
temptation of Eve becomes a seduction described in
copulatory terms familiar to the reader who recalls
Milton's description of the serpent which

Addressed his way: not with indented
wave
Prone on the ground, as since, but on his rear,
Circular base of rising folds, that towered
Fold above fold, a surging maze . . .
With burnished neck of verdant gold, erect
Amidst his circling spires . . .

(*Paradise Lost,* Book IX, ll. 496–502)

To this serpent Thomas adds a prehensile tail which is
coiled around the trunk of the forbidden tree, thus en-
abling that old worm, tumescent with evil, to mount
Eve.

The word "butt" carries a variety of meanings: the
wether is the butt of the worm. The climbing grave is a
mound of earth, a butt, of Calvary. Adam's wether,
Christ, becomes the butt or target of abuse as the result
of the Fall. The wether with its horns thrusts down or
butts the serpent to redeem man. "Horned down with
skullfoot and the skull of toes" reverses the action in
the previous line in which the serpent climbed the tree
and made of Christ the butt of mankind. Now Christ,
through his sacrifice, butts the serpent or horns it down,
by mounting the Cross. Donne expresses the same
thought in his sonnet "Ascension":

O strong Ramme, which hast batter'd heaven
for mee,
Mild Lambe, which with thy blood, hast
mark'd the path; . . .

The lamb, ram, wether are at once the sufferer, avenger,
redeemer of mankind. "Skullfoot" is a compressed image

36

which evokes the figure of a barefoot Christ climbing
a skull-shaped hill to the place of execution, treading
down death, triumphing over the "climbing grave."
"Skullfoot" is derived from the Gospel description of
the place of crucifixion: Golgotha is a Hebrew word for
skull. Calvary is its equivalent from the Latin *calvaria*,
a skull, a translation of the Greek word *kranion*. In the
King James Bible three Gospels mention Golgotha
(Matthew, Mark, and John), but the Gospel of Luke
speaks of Calvary.[6]

The hill received its name according to one legend
because it was a place of execution and therefore was
known as the hill of skulls.[7] Another legend tells of
Noah, who preserved the Tree of Knowledge and the
bones of Adam, later dividing these relics among his
three sons. The skull was given to Shem, who buried it
on a hill in Judea, the very hill, as the legend tells us,
on which Christ was crucified. Noah himself planted on
Mount Lebanon the tree of which the Cross was made.[8]
Modern interpretation holds that the place was called
the skull because of the shape of the hill.

"Skullfoot" may also refer to God's curse upon the
serpent: "it [woman's seed] shall bruise thy head"
(Genesis 3:15–16). Milton describes this final triumph
promised in Genesis:

> When Jesus, son of Mary, second Eve . . .
> Then rising from his grave,
> Spoiled Principalities and Powers, triumphed
> In open show, and, with ascension bright,
> Captivity led captive through the Air
> The realm of Satan, long usurped,
> Whom he shall tread at last under our
>   feet, . . .
>   (*Paradise Lost*, Book X, ll. 183–190)

In his magnificent poem on the Crucifixion, *The Christ
of Velázquez*, Miguel de Unamuno paraphrases Genesis
3:15, echoes Milton, and foreshadows Thomas in a strik-
ingly similar image:

37

and Thou, the Man elevated to God,
who art forever triumphant, Thou wast
crushing his skull with the foot of Thy cross.[9]

After "skullfoot," why "skull of toes"? The image is
not new; it appears in one of Thomas's early poems:
"From poles of skull and toe the windy blood."[10] The
only explanation that can be offered is that the phrase
is an extension and repetition of "skullfoot," suggesting
a walking skull or a walking death. Or perhaps it is a
pun on the curse "bruise thy head" (stubbed toes
against skull). The toe-stubbing image has its counter-
part in an anecdote related by St. John Chrysostom in
his *Encomium on St. John the Baptist*. It is not likely
that Thomas knew this work of the golden-mouthed
Church Father (translated from a Coptic text by E. A.
Wallis Budge), but I offer the quotation as an interest-
ing example of coincidence:

> Now at the time when the cataclysm of waters in-
> creased upon the earth in the days of Noah, the
> trees and the waters of the flood rolled over the
> body of Adam, and they carried it away and de-
> posited it in the midst of Jerusalem, and the waters
> of the earth flowed over it and covered it. And
> when the Saviour had come and He was walking
> about that place, and was teaching, saying, 'If any
> man serveth Me My Father shall pay him honor;
> My Father, deliver Me from this hour'—at the very
> moment when the Saviour said these things the
> toe-nail of His right foot struck the head of Adam.
> And thus far is the story.[11]

"On thunderous pavements in the garden time" car-
ries out Thomas's intention of contracting, as Milton
does, all tenses into one. As in *Paradise Lost* Milton
moves on four levels simultaneously: present, past,
future, and eternity; so Thomas merges the temptation,
the Fall, and the Redemption into one single instant.
His imagery is derived from two different Biblical in-
cidents separated in time; yet consequence and cause
(in that order) are fused into the one line which tells

us of the momentous event in Eden ("garden time")
when the Fall implied the Atonement. The moment in
which Eve ate the apple and the ninth hour in which
Christ yielded up his spirit are one in time, for the
"thunderous pavements" were heard long before "the
veil of the temple was rent in twain from the top to
the bottom; and the earth did quake, and the rocks
rent" (Matthew 27:51). It is possible that "thunderous
pavements" is an allusion to the reverberation of the
mob's shouts before Pilate's judgment seat.

> When Pilate therefore heard that saying, he
> brought Jesus forth, and sat down in the judgment
> seat in a place that is called the Pavement . . .
> And he saith . . . Behold your King! But they
> cried out away with him.
>
> (John 19:13–15)

The next four lines introduce the second theme, the
Incarnation, moving quickly in bold, ironic, irreverent
imagery. After the historical introduction of Eden and
Golgotha, God speaks. "Rip of the vaults" he calls him-
self, and completes his identity by repeating his full
name, Rip Van Winkle of the heavenly vaults ("windy
salvages"). He is the long-bearded Ancient of Days who
stirs from his timeless cradle, feels the desire to beget
himself, and prepares to descend to one of the daughters
of men. This image of God the Father seems to have
been fashioned out of Washington Irving's *Sketch-Book*
and Blake's illustrations from the *Book of Urizen* and
Song of Los. The time has come for God to beget him-
self as his Son to "bruise the head of the serpent" so that
his own prophecy may be fulfilled. The Word is ready
to descend from the timeless "windy salvages" to a cra-
dle in time. Divinity now prepares to clothe itself in
mortality. A series of phallic images follows. This is an
anthropomorphic God, an old man ("Old cock from
nowheres . . . with bones unbuttoned") who reaches
for his marrow-ladle, the celestial phallus, stored in the
"wrinkled undertaker's van," the ancient divine loins
which are to beget life destined for death.

39

The last quatrain has a threefold purpose: (1) In its return to ovine imagery it binds the sonnet together by merging the themes of sacrifice and incarnation into a single zodiacal image. (2) The reintroduction of spring completes not only the birth-death-resurrection cycle but the cycle of the seasons as well. (3) It is a description of the simultaneous action of generation and regeneration: the supernatural phenomenon of God begetting a son is reflected in the natural phenomenon of the earth regenerating itself in the spring. The first two lines of the quatrain: "The black ram, shuffling of the year old winter / Alone alive among his mutton fold," are a modified version of a line in the unpublished Thomas poem quoted above: "The black sheep, shuffling of the fold, old winter." Aries, the Ram of Spring, becomes the black ram of winter in Thomas's zodiacal system, transformed by a remembered line from *Othello:* "An old black ram is tupping your white ewe." [12] "Shuffling of the year" and "old winter" are synonyms of "black ram." The zodiacal ram of spring, alive and potent among his ewes, is a vigorous contrast to the paschal lamb, marked for slaughter in the same season. [13]

Remaining apart as witnesses to the drama of regeneration are the antipodean points in the globe recording two full solar cycles. Spring chimes twice: once for a natural event, the equinoctial birth of the year on March 22, and once for a supernatural event on March 25 (the Annunciation and Incarnation). The chiming of the seasons is a repetition of a bell-pulling image in an earlier poem, "I see the boys of summer in their ruin," where Thomas describes seasonal changes:

But seasons must be challenged or they totter
Into a chiming quarter
When, punctual as death, we ring the stars;
There, in his night, the black-tongued bells
The sleepy man of winter pulls
Nor blows back moon-and-midnight as she
    blows. [14]

The zodiacal circle becomes a ladder in line 13 because zodiacal signs are described as ascending and descending. Yielding to an opportunity to pun: rung (ladder) and rung (chimed), Thomas manages also to establish a consistent motif of the ladder: the solar metaphor of descent and ascent (Capricorn and Cancer) in the first sonnet, and the reference to Jacob's dream of angels ascending and descending the ladder ("rung . . . Jacob to the stars") in the second sonnet. The ladder in the third sonnet is clearly a solar image. I assume that Thomas knew something about the symbol of the ladder in Egyptian solar myths, since his ninth sonnet reveals a knowledge of Egyptian myth and funerary customs. We learn in J. H. Breasted's *The Dawn of Conscience* that "The ladder leading to the sky was originally an element of the Solar faith." [15] E. A. W. Budge, in his *Osiris and the Egyptian Resurrection*, quotes an entire passage from the Pyramid Texts which begins with an apostrophe to the ladder: "Homage to thee O Ladder of the God!" and concludes with a reference to a heavenly ascent by means of the ladder: ". . . he appeareth in heaven on the Ladder of the God." [16]

A reading of the 114th Psalm, Milton's "On the Morning of Christ's Nativity," and Thomas's third sonnet will reveal that the Psalmist and the poets attempted to achieve the same purpose: the description of Nature's response to an event in time. The Psalmist describes Nature in awe at the momentous liberation of Israel from Egypt; Milton reflects the exultation of Nature in the joyful prodigy of the Nativity; and Thomas records the ringing of the antipodes at the moment of the Incarnation. The Psalmist sang of mountains trembling and seas receding:

> The sea saw it, and fled: Jordan was driven
> back.
> The mountains skipped like rams
> and the little hills like lambs.

Milton ranges not only through comparative mythology

to sing his jubilation (there are three stanzas alone on Isis, Osiris, and Typhon), but he also moves through seas, antipodes, and heavens to describe in vast panoramas the awe in which Nature stood before "that glorious Form." Milton is as aware of Nature's creativity as Thomas is, and he does not hesitate to describe, in sexual imagery, the processes of generation. Nature, Milton tells us, knew that

> It was no season then for her
> To wanton with the Sun her lusty Paramour.
>
> (ll. 35–36)

Thomas's imagery is as sexual as Milton's as he speaks of the union of earth and sun in the language of the zodiac. Thomas's imagery of solar myth in the last four lines of the sonnet matches the emphasis which Milton places on the sun in his poem, varying the sun image at least five times. Milton does not forget, in his youthful, learned piety, that the Nativity coincided with and supplanted the festival of the winter solstice and the Saturnalia which celebrated it. Nor does Thomas forget that the Incarnation coincides with the spring equinox.

Both Milton and Thomas are attuned to the universal strain. Milton commands the heavens to echo the music of the angels, "Harping in loud and solemn quire," and he exhorts the spheres to sound their "ninefold harmony":

> Ring out ye Crystal sphears,
> Once bless our human ears,
>   (If ye have power to touch our senses so)
> And let your silver chime
> Move in melodious time;
>   And let the Base of Heavn's deep Organ
>   blow,
> And with your ninefold harmony
> Make up full consort to th' Angelike sym-
>   phony.
>
> (ll. 124–132)

And Thomas, in a language which suggests a xylophone

image (ladder-like in form, bell-like in sound), describes the antipodes ringing variations on the theme of procreation. Like Milton's "silver chime," spring chimes twice to signal a prodigious event in time.

4

Sonnet IV

> . . . and no man knoweth who the Son is, but the Father;
> and who the Father is, but the Son . . .
>
> > Luke 10:22

> 1st Doctor: Another question I ask you yet
> > You said one of these three took flesh and blood
> > And she a clean maid. I cannot believe it.
> > Clean maid and mother never yet in one person
> > stood.
> >
> > > from "Christ and the Doctors,"
> > > *Ludus Coventriae* (ll. 178–187)

WHEN WE REACH the fourth sonnet we are confronted,
for the first and only time in the sequence, by interroga-
tions: six riddles and two derisive, taunting questions.
We might feel about these riddles as Alice does about
the Hatter's remark, that it "seemed to her to have no
sort of meaning in it, and yet it was certainly English." [1]
There is always the nagging suspicion that these riddles
might have been asked by Thomas in the same manner
that the Hatter put his riddle to Alice ("Why is a raven
like a writing-desk?") and then have offered, when
asked to give the answer, the Hatter's reply: "I haven't
the slightest idea." [2] It is not so much the answers that
are important as the question the reader poses: Why
are these questions here? There are no answers to the
riddles. The answers to the questions in the octave are

44

implied in the questions themselves. The purpose of these riddles may offer the reader one of two possibilities. He may sigh wearily as Alice does and feel that Dylan Thomas might have done "something better with the time than wasting it in asking riddles that have no answers." Or he may, by careful examination of the sequence, arrive at a reason for the presence of the riddles. The first choice is an easy one and makes of Thomas as rude a man as is the Hatter—and more, it makes of him a charlatan. He was neither rude to his readers, nor a charlatan in his craft. One recalls Socrates in his offer to Ion: "Which do you prefer to be thought, dishonest or inspired?" And Ion's choice: "There is a great difference, Socrates, between them; and inspiration is the far nobler alternative." [3] I have assumed that alternative for Dylan Thomas.

The fourth sonnet is preceded by the sonnet in which God declares his intention to become man; and it is followed by the sonnet of the Annunciation. Chronologically, the thematic content of the fourth sonnet should place it after the fifth; but Thomas is bound neither by theology nor chronology. Theologically he might stand condemned as a heretic: he might be a Sabellian, an Adoptionist, an Arian; chronologically he remains the despair of any reader who measures time by clock and calendar. Thomas does not observe a sequential scheme in the first seven sonnets; it is only in the last three sonnets that he establishes a progressive movement from time into eternity. The first sonnet gives us the Nativity, the second describes the child growing, the third goes back to the Incarnation as divine intention, the fourth gives us the Nativity again.

In Renaissance depictions of the episodes in Christ's life we are aware of the anachronistic dress of the figures in the painting: Mary appears in rich warm velvets against a background of Renaissance interiors as if she were the wife of a Venetian magnifico rather than the wife of a Nazarene carpenter. So in this poem the epi-

45

sodes contain imagery that is deliberately anachronistic. The first sonnet makes use of journalistic metaphors, describing, in a poetic hypothesis, newspaper headlines announcing the Nativity. In the fourth sonnet Thomas returns to journalistic imagery and creates a scene composed of careful substitutions for the familiar setting of the first Christmas. There are no shepherds here, nor are there Wise Men; instead, there seem to be reporters and photographers come to ask riddles of the principals of this unusual event. The rapid, staccato barrage of riddles suggests impatient, literal-minded pressmen crowding the manger, eager to obtain a statement, a fact, a photograph.[4]

The sonnet begins with a set of enigma variations or the chain question, a type of riddle in which one question leads to another, each one impossible to answer.[5] There are five riddles asked in rapid succession, and I believe they are addressed to the infant prodigy as if he were a quiz kid who could dazzle the expectant world with his encyclopedic knowledge. The first riddle is ironic: the wordless Word is asked to give the meter of the dictionary, in which we learn that "infant" originally meant "unable to speak." [6] The next question introduces a chain of biological riddles. The dimensions of genesis are asked for so that a curious world might know the statistics of the Incarnation. The question everyone asks upon hearing of the birth of a child is whether it is a boy or a girl; this is the next question, posed in the vocabulary of electricity ("short spark's gender") with implied sexual connotations. And since the language is that of an electrical device, the word "gender" is appropriate: it suggests the designation of parts referred to as "male" or "female" by electricians. The last of the triad of biological riddles deals with morphology: How can a spirit (shade) "without shape" beget a child of flesh? And since this prodigy is himself shape and shade, he would know the answer. The next riddle may have an answer. The "shape of Pharaoh's echo" [7] is an obelisk,

46

a monolithic echo of the achievements of his reign. What the obelisk originally signified is still unknown, but, as E. A. W. Budge remarks in the *Guide to the Egyptian Collections in the British Museum,* ". . . it is probable that they were connected with a solar, or even phallic cult, but as the texts afford no explanation of their meaning it is useless to theorize." [8] Thomas did not have to go to the banks of the Nile to see an obelisk. Cleopatra's Needle stands on the Victoria Embankment of the Thames,[9] and Thomas must have seen it as early as 1933, the year in which he moved to London.[10] The phallic significance of the obelisk is consistent with the central theme of this sonnet: the mysterious paternity of the child in the manger.

The questions are halted by the child's unspoken parenthetical aside. The wordless infant ("shape of age") attempts to answer in "a wounded whisper," and yet he remains silent. The wounded whisper is an anticipation of the wounded cry from the Cross, when the son will ask the Father a question: "Why hast Thou forsaken me?"

The last question, in the form of a mathematical riddle, seems to be a nonsense riddle, but it is the kind of nonsense theologians argue about. The "burning gentry" may refer to the inhabitants of Sodom and Gomorrah whose sinfulness was so combustibly punished. The fanciful portion of a sixth of wind which "blew out the burning gentry" suggests that God fanned the flames with a fraction of the divine whirlwind. "Blew out" may also mean destroyed, not extinguished. Thomas has Biblical meteorological data to draw from for apportionment of winds. The Book of Enoch in the Pseudepigrapha divides and numbers the winds:

> . . . And there mine eyes saw the secrets . . . of the winds, how they are divided to blow over the earth.
>
> (41:3)
> And at the end of the earth I saw portals from

47

which the winds go forth and blow over the earth
. . . through four of these [portals] come winds
of blessing and prosperity, and from those eight
[portals] come hurtful winds . . .

(76: 1–5)

Thomas, too, has fixed upon twelve winds as an even
dozen, for in at least four of his poems he speaks
of "twelve winds," "twelve-winded circles," "twelve-
winded marrow," "twelve triangles of the cherub
winds."[11] Thomas has poetic as well as Biblical prece-
dent for his heavenly fractions. Milton counts one-third
of the angelic host as defectors from Heaven. Satan's
logistics are revealed in scorn to Abdiel, a loyal angel,

. . . durst oppose
A third part of the gods, in synod met
Their deities to assert . . .

(*Paradise Lost*, Book VI, ll. 156–159)

Why Thomas chooses one-sixth of wind, I do not know.
Nor am I certain, however tempting it is to assume, that
the "burning gentry" are inhabitants of the Cities of the
Plain. Rather do I think that they may be the damned
angels blown out, expelled, as Milton describes them,
plummeting to perdition:

Hurled headlong flaming from the ethereal
sky,
With hideous ruin and combustion . . .

(*Paradise Lost*, Book I, ll. 44–45)

Perhaps the interrogators in the fourth sonnet believe
that the child can offer information about the windy
ordnance of heaven, or at least a fraction thereof.

The second unspoken parenthetical aside is the child's
comment upon the questions which, like the interroga-
tion mark following them, are so many misshapen,
hunchbacked punctuation symbols of doubt and uncer-
tainty compared with the exclamation point, that obe-
lisk of suddenness and command, the "poker marrow,"
the agent of the divine intention to become flesh. The

sestet ends the interrogation of the child by the reporters, who now turn to Mary.

In the octave the interrogators become inquisitors. The two questions asked are taunting, mocking questions about the paternity of the child. To the minds of shepherds the Incarnation was not a complex event beyond credibility. Being assured by the angel of the Lord, they were no longer afraid but hurried to Bethlehem to find a babe wrapped in swaddling clothes in a manger. They asked no questions but repeated what the angel had said to them about this child. Mary, listening quietly to the shepherds, pondered their words. Nor did Simeon and Anna the prophetess ask any questions. But the inquisitors in this sonnet ask incredulously and derisively whether a scarecrow made of bamboo poles ("bamboo man among your acres") had fathered this child. For them it is as ludicrous to believe that Mary had conceived of the Holy Spirit as it would be to believe her had she pointed to the scarecrow as the father. "Your acres," is a nasty, obscene metaphor referring not only to Mary's body but to a field where a farm hand might have lurked, waiting for Mary. The bamboo image serves Thomas well, since bamboo stalks are hollow and jointed, suggesting "old cock from nowheres . . . with bones unbuttoned" of the first sonnet and the "hollow agent" of the second sonnet.[12] The next question is cruel: Mary is asked whether she tried to conceal the pregnancy by corseting the "boneyards." The "crooked boy" is the child in the womb, the inverted question mark, the shape of the embryo, the result of the "poker marrow." The "boneyards," slang for cemetery, is a metaphor of Mary's body, the source of life as well as death for the child. The disbelief among the inquisitors persists in the menacing taunt of "Button your bodice." Mary is warned that, try as she will to conceal this child, the inquisitors will find him out. "Hump of splinters" is a cruelly consistent metaphor of the child, reminding us that the father was a "bamboo man." Pun and Biblical parable combine in the warning of the camel's eye needling through the shroud. Mary's body and garments, protective of the child, are described as a shroud. The wounded whisper, the splinters, and the shroud are the vocabulary of disaster, prefiguring the Crucifixion in the eighth sonnet.

The skepticism of the Child's paternity expressed by the inquisitors in this sonnet finds a parallel in an old ballad called "The Cherry-Tree Carol," which was derived from an episode in the Apocryphal Gospel of Pseudo-Matthew (Chapter 20):

> Joseph and Mary walked
>   through an orchard green,
> Where was berries and cherries
>   as thick as might be seen.
>
> O then bespoke Mary
>   so meek and so mild:
> 'Pluck me one cherry, Joseph,
>   for I am with child.'
>
> O then bespoke Joseph,
>   with words most unkind:
> 'Let him pluck thee a cherry
>   that brought thee with child.' [13]

A more extended instance of skepticism of Christ's paternity is found in the Book of James or Protevangelion of the New Testament Apocrypha:

> Now it was in the sixth month with her, and behold Joseph came from his building [carpentry] and he entered into his house and found her great with child. And he smote his face and cast himself down upon the ground on sackcloth and wept bitterly, saying: With what countenance shall I look unto the Lord my God: and what prayer shall I make concerning this maiden: for I received her out of the temple of the Lord my God a virgin, and have

50

not kept her safe. Who is he that hath ensnared me? Who hath done this evil in mine house and hath defiled the Virgin:

(13:1)

Joseph and Mary are then brought before the priest and the assembly and are questioned:

And the priest said: Mary, wherefore hast thou done this, and wherefore hast thou humbled thy soul and forgotten the Lord thy God, thou that wast nurtured in the Holy of Holies and didst receive food at the hand of an angel and didst hear the hymns and didst dance before the Lord, wherefore hast thou done this?

But she wept bitterly, saying: As the Lord my God liveth I am pure before him and I know not a man.

(15:2, 3) [14]

Another instance of skepticism, as harsh as that in the sonnet, occurs in the Gospel of Nicodemus (2:3, 4) in the New Testament Apocrypha. Two groups of elders dispute each other, before Pilate, over Christ's paternity. One group insists: "Thou wert born of fornication"; and the other group counters with: "We say not that he came of fornication; but we know that Joseph was betrothed unto Mary, and he was not born of fornication."

Whether Thomas knew of these Apocryphal Gospels, I cannot say with certainty. I think he knew the "Cherry-Tree Carol," and I am certain that he knew Buck Mulligan's "Ballad of Joking Jesus" in *Ulysses,* a line of which must have occurred to him as he wrote these sonnets: "My mother's a jew, my father's a bird." [15]

The last five lines of the sonnet are developed out of photography and moving-picture imagery. The "camel's eye" (camera's eye) is the photographer's camera, and the shroud is the black focusing cloth which he drapes shroudlike, over himself and his camera. There are two simultaneous reflections in the concluding quatrain: the

51

reflection of the infant in his mother's eyes as she looks at him lovingly, and the reflection of mother and child in the lens of the camera focused on the Nativity scene. The "mushroom features" may be the whitish-pink face of the infant, its head surrounded by a traditional nimbus suggesting the detached crown of a mushroom. "Mushroom features" may also be the enlargement of the features as seen by a photographer through a focusing glass, a device which magnifies the image.

The setting in the last four lines conveys an impression of photographers arranging a posed scene of mother and child, of stable beasts, and of adoring shepherds for the next day's tabloid ("tomorrow's scream"). The vocabulary in the quatrain is a glossary of photographic terms. Stills are snapped at night in the grain fields of Bethlehem, "the bread-sided field." One can almost hear the photographers' instructions: "Once more, a close-up, smile." The once smiling faces, caught in a close-up, will be framed in the wall of pictures, among the records of other episodes such as the Presentation in the temple, or Jesus at the age of twelve among the doctors in the temple.

The last four lines also effect a contrast to the scene of the Nativity by anticipating the future in the contemporary imagery of photography. The Nativity in this sonnet is intruded upon by a world eager for a sign, searching with arc lamps and floodlights. But the record of that event, the "stills snapped at night" by the light of arc lamps, is seen as a superfluous collection of films discarded on the cutting-room floor by an editor indifferent to the meaning of the Nativity ("thrown back upon the cutting flood"). But to Mary the "close-up . . . in the wall of pictures" will be a reminder in later years that the Nativity was the only time of warmth and safety for her son. She will behold him again, but not among wonder-struck shepherds and adoring Magi. She who looked down upon him in the manger will look up at him on the Cross in the agonizing exchange of "love's reflection." The lines, then, describe two attitudes—that of the indifferent chronicler (the photography editor) and that of Mary.

The vocabulary of photography in the last four lines is confusing, particularly the term "cutting flood." One at once suspects a pun: if the arc in "arc-lamped" suggested to Thomas the rainbow arc, Noah's ark, and the Flood by an associational process, we have an instance of an overextended pun. As I see it, the manger animals, the star of the Nativity, and the New Covenant fuse with arc lamps and floodlights to give Thomas his pun. There is also the possibility that the cutting or editing of photographic film, with its prodigal rejection of footage and "shots" thrown on the cutting-room floor, suggested to Thomas the combination of cutting floor with floodlights, giving him "cutting flood."

Did Thomas, in his careful arrangement of the Nativity scene for filming, suggest that in the incandescence of arc lamps and the glare of floodlights the light of the world was not seen? And did he, in his deliberate choice of words, realize that "thrown back" is the literal meaning of rejected? And knowing that, is it possible that he paraphrased, in those two words, St. John's testimony?

That was the true Light, which lighteth every man that cometh into the world. He was in the world, and the world was made by him, and the world knew him not. He came unto his own, and his own received him not.

(John 1:9, 10)

5

Sonnet V

Then said Mary unto the angel, How shall this be, seeing
I know not a man?

Luke 1:34

These cards are in touch with a thing I'll show you at
Christmas . . .

Charles Williams,
The Greater Trumps, p. 54

THE FIFTH SONNET moves in centrifugal confusion be-
tween two fixed points: the Annunciation in the open-
ing line and the Nativity in the last two lines. There is
an implicit time span of nine months, from March 25
to December 25; there is a suggestion of polar wastes
and parched deserts; and there are familiar Biblical and
literary characters masked by incongruous epithets. Be-
tween the descent of Gabriel and the prophetic ut-
terance of the white bear, seasons, persons, places, and
events swirl in a madly shaken kaleidoscope. Out of the
centrifugal motion of his imagery Thomas manages, by
an inexplicable torsion, to force his images into centrip-
etal direction toward a central theme. The dynamics in
this sonnet are a combination of a volcanic eruption and
a polar maelstrom. Three events—Gabriel's annuncia-
tion, a hazardous journey, and a nativity—are described
in imagery of playing cards, literature, the Bible, and
the sea.

54

The tone of the sonnet is that of a sermon preached by an itinerant, bibulous evangelist in a homely parable. The first line begins with a connective particle, so frequent in the Bible; and there is a false hymnal quality suggested by "Jesu's," a vocative curiously in the possessive case.[1] The use of the verb "slew" in "slew my hunger" has pseudo-Biblical overtones, although it is more suggestive of killing a thirst. And, finally, the sustained parable points to a kinship between this sonnet and the sermon on Jonah preached by Father Mapple in *Moby Dick*.[2]

The playing card images recall Hugh Latimer's "Sermons on the Card" preached in Cambridge in December, 1529. In these sermons Bishop Latimer used the card-playing games of the Christmas season as his parable. His language was drawn from the trump card and from the rules of primero, the favorite card game of the students. Here are a few examples of Latimer's language:

> And whereas you are wont to celebrate Christmas in playing at cards, I intend, by God's grace, to deal unto you Christ's cards, wherein you shall perceive Christ's role. The game that we will play at shall be called the triumph, which, if it be well played at, he that dealeth shall win; the players shall likewise win; and the standers and lookers upon shall do the same; insomuch that there is no man that is willing to play at this triumph with these cards, but they shall be all winners, and no losers.
>
> Now turn up your trump, your heart (hearts is trump, as I said before), and cast your trump, your heart, on this card . . .[3]

The mystery of the Annunciation is described in sonnet V in the language of a Hollywood scenario. This is no hermaphroditic angel, no draped figure with flowing hair whose sex is ambiguous. The masculinity of Gabriel is established at once. He appears in a sudden sweep before Mary, not as God's deputy with a lily or scepter in his right hand and an *Ave Maria* on his lips. He breezes in from the windy West as a cowboy with two guns and a deck of stacked cards. There is no beating of wings before the startled maiden; instead, we almost hear the slap of leather holsters against angelic thighs. Perhaps the gun-toting archangel is equipped for a possible encounter with that bad eminence, Satan, who might be lurking somewhere in the heavenly plains. That there are armed angels should come as no surprise to those who know Michael as the warrior angel with brandished sword, or Gabriel as the armed guardian, posted by Milton outside the gates of Paradise. Thomas's image is bizarre and the rhythm of the verse syncopated (the alliteratives are deliberate) because it is exactly the sensational device a spellbinding evangelist would use to arrest the attention of his listeners. There is an ironic reservation implicit in the entire setting of this version of the Annunciation, to be atoned for later in the concluding lines. There is neither veneration here, nor wonder, nor tenderness such as we find in the Annunciation poems of Donne, Rilke, and Yeats.[4]

The play on Sir Walter Scott's line "Oh! Young Lochinvar is come out of the west" hints at Thomas's interpretation of the Annunciation: the bride whose troth has been plighted to Joseph is carried off by no mere mortal, but by God himself. There is an echo, too, of a Shropshire folk rhyme:

> There were 3 Angels com from the west
> The one brot fire and the other brot frost
> The other brot the book of Jesus Christ
> In the name of the Father, and of the Son,
>   and of the Holy Ghost.[5]

We do not hear the annunciation which puzzled Mary:

> And behold, thou shalt conceive in thy womb, and bring forth a son, and shallt call his name Jesus. He shall be great; and shall be called the Son of

the Highest; and the Lord God shall give unto him the throne of his father David: And he shall reign over the house of Jacob forever; and of his Kingdom there shall be no end.

(Luke 1:31–33)

This Gabriel is an angel not of words but of gesture. He tells Mary's fortune with a pack of cards produced in a parlor-trick flourish from the sleeve of Jesus. The sleeve image poses a theological problem: how can Jesus be present at the Annunciation before he is born? John Donne was not perplexed by such an impossibility. In his "Annunciation" (of the *Holy Sonnets*) Donne addresses Mary:

Ere by the spheres time was created, thou
Wast in his mind, who is thy Son, and Brother;

Thomas's concern here is not theology but legerdemain. The archangel is a cardsharp, and a sleeve is usually the source of card tricks and surprises.[6] Much that occurs in the first four lines is a mixture of parable, metaphor, and pun. Christ's garment for which the soldiers cast lots on Calvary is a seamless coat. That it was a type of sleeveless garment is a detail which is not important to Thomas. What is important is that the coat suggests the sleeve, and the sleeve the card trick. The cards Thomas describes are a king, jacks, and a queen, known as coat cards because the figures are clad in coats. A corruption of the term "coat" has given us "court" cards—etymologically incorrect but royally consistent with the figures on the cards.

"Trumped up" is packed with several meanings: the cards are trump cards; the cards are slipped out of a sleeve; the cards are stacked against Jesus because of trumped-up charges against him; "trumped" also suggests the millennial function of Gabriel: he is the angel of the last trump on the Day of Judgment. The cards themselves reveal that poet and angelic emissary are clever dealers. Like Pope, in his detailed description of omber in "The Rape of the Lock," Thomas chooses his

57

cards knowingly. He may care little about soterial and sartorial matters such as Jesus' sleeve, but he pays close attention to his cards. Obviously Gabriel is not playing poker: the suit he picks is not a royal flush, nor a straight. If it were any card game consistent with the outcome of the Annunciation, it would be mort, a macabre-named variety of whist in which there are three players and a dummy (God, Gabriel as dealer, and Mary, with Christ as the dummy or dead hand). The cards foretell disaster. The term "spots" is used in connection with any card from ten to two; all other cards from ace to jack are designated by their suit. Thomas has deliberately chosen to speak of the "King of spots" because it is Christ's card. I do not think he means king of spades. The "King of spots" designates the thorn-crowned king with five spots or stigmata. The jacks are the two cruci-fied thieves (knaves) "sheath-decked" or wrapped in shrouds. And the "queen with the shuffled heart" is Mary, whose heart will be pierced by her Son's agony.[7]

Is the "fake gentleman" Gabriel in disguise? Is he a fake because he is a fraud, or is he a fake because he has assumed the disguise of a "suit of spades"? Does he come to Mary clad in apparel appropriate to his role as announcer of a birth which will end in a humiliating death? Is he as amusing a figure as the animated cards in *Alice's Adventures in Wonderland,* or is he as fatal as the Queen of Spades in Pushkin's story? There is something of the ridiculous about this gun-bearing arch-angel, clad in one of Thomas's puns; but there is some-thing of the sinister, too. The spade, in playing cards, is an emblem derived from the Spanish *espada* (sword); in fortunetelling the spade is the symbol of death. Thirty-three years after Gabriel's Annunciation Mary will see her son's side pierced by a soldier's spear.

Thomas is not the only interpreter of the Annuncia-tion who has disguised Gabriel. Saint Ephrem, a fourth-century Eastern Father, believed that "the Archangel Gabriel was sent under the form of a venerable aged

58

man lest so chaste and modest a maiden should be troubled, or seized with any fear, at a youthful appearance." [8] Rilke's angel has "a face of a young man" (*der Engel, eines Jünglings Ausgesicht*) which reflects the fright of Mary: both archangel and Virgin are overwhelmed by fear.[9] But Thomas's Gabriel is not concerned about Mary's comfort, nor does he share her fear. This Gabriel is an emissary who leaves Mary with no illusions. The cards do not lie. In Luke's version Gabriel makes no mention of the grief to come. In a fifteenth-century lyric dialogue between Christ and Mary ("Dear Son, Leave Thy Weeping"), we hear Mary's bitter complaint:

> Christ: 'Also, modyre, there schall a speyre
> My tendure hert all to-teyre;
> The blud schall keuyre my body ther
> Gret rwthe yt schall be to see.
>
> Mary: 'A! dere sone, that is a heavy cas;
> When Gabrell cnellyd before my face,
> And sayd "heylle lady full of grace"
> He never told me noothing of this.' [10]

In Thomas's poem she is silent, aware at once that this Annunciation makes of her body her son's grave. Thomas implies the paradox which Donne describes in his "The Annunciation and Passion: Upon the Annunciation and Passion falling upon one day":

> Her Maker put to making, and the head
> Of life, at once, not yet alive, yet dead . . .
>
> At once a Sonne is promised her, and gone,
> Gabriell gives Christ to her, He her to John;

The fake gentleman, having performed his task as agent of the Annunciation, is carried away by the momentum of his prophecy; propelled as he is by the winds from the west, the winds of fertility and death.[11] If he is the angel announcing the Incarnation, he is also the angel who will sound the Resurrection with his two

six-shooters, signaling the end with a bang. From for-
tunetelling by cards, he now turns to conjuring, and
with the eloquence of a side-show barker he produces,
in a grammatical nightmare of asyntactical pronouns,
his Biblical performers.

That this sonnet may be an evangelist's parable is
borne out by the shift in pronouns, the montage effect of
merging deserts and seas, and the mixture of Biblical
and literary personalities. The evangelist himself is prob-
ably tipsy from salvation's bottle, and is freed, there-
fore, from the limits of logic, time, and distance. The
shift from third person ("the fake gentleman") to "my
Byzantine Adam" to "I fell" is a dramatic device of the
narrator to impress his listeners by impersonating the
Biblical characters. The contents of the next lines are
based on the parallel themes of gestation and Biblical
narrative.

The Biblical verse "And Abraham rose early in the
morning, and took bread, and a bottle of water, and
gave it to Hagar . . ." (Genesis 21:14) is not so com-
pletely transformed that we cannot recognize the source
of "Rose my Byzantine Adam in the night." Early morn-
ing becomes night, Abraham is changed to Adam, and
the bottle of water becomes the bottle of salvation. This
Adam, rising in the night, reminds us of the second
Adam who comes "like the day of the Lord as a thief
in the night" (I Thessalonians 5:2). It is in this same
epistle (5:6, 7) that we find St. Paul's exhortation to re-
main awake and sober, a necessary state for the Byzan-
tine Adam, too:

> Therefore let us not sleep as do others; but let us
> watch and be sober.
> For they that sleep sleep in the night; and they that
> be drunken are drunken in the night.

The privations of Christ's forty-day fast in the desert
and the sustenance he received from ministering angels
may have suggested the image of wastelands and nour-
ishing mushrooms in the following lines. In that case
"Byzantine" may describe the gaunt, emaciated figures

of Aramaean motif in the Byzantine iconography of the Eastern Church, which Thomas may have seen in reproductions or museums. But if Thomas had read Procopius or Gibbon, the epithet might have come to mean Oriental sensuality or unbridled lusts to him. It is difficult to determine whether Thomas had Jesus or Justinian in mind. And it is equally difficult to decide whether Byzantine Adam is lustful, gauntly penitent, or even archetypically nocturnal. The lines which follow suggest that perhaps new wine in the old Adam was more than he could hold. God-intoxicated and black-tongued (the latter condition caused by thirst, hangover, or pellagra), Adam begins a perilous journey.

If this Adam is a penitential Adam, then portions in this sonnet are traceable to a source which I have mentioned before: the Pseudepigrapha of the Old Testament. Eve is the narrator of the quest for penance described in the Books of Adam and Eve:

> And we sat together before the gate of paradise. Adam weeping with his face bent down to the earth, lay on the ground lamenting. And seven days passed by and we had nothing to eat and were consumed with great hunger, and I Eve cried with a loud voice: 'Pity me, O Lord, My Creator; for my sake Adam suffereth thus!'
>
> (28:1–2)
>
> And I said to Adam: 'Rise up! my lord, that we may seek us food; for now my spirit faileth me and my heart within me is brought low.'
>
> (29:1–2)
>
> And Adam arose and we roamed through all lands and found nothing to eat save nettles (and) grass of the field. And we returned again to the gates of paradise and cried aloud and entreated: 'Have compassion on thy creature. O Lord Creator, allow us food.'
>
> (30:1–2)
>
> And Adam came to Jordan and he entered into the water and he plunged himself altogether into the

flood, even (to) the hairs of his head, while he made supplication to God and sent (up) prayers to Him.

(36:4)

If the Adam who rises in the night is archetypically nocturnal, he is a voyager who has undertaken a hazardous night journey by water, a symbolic quest for rebirth or redemption. He is the forerunner of Nicodemus, who comes to Jesus at night to be told "Except a man be born of the water and of the spirit, he cannot enter the Kingdom of God" (John 3:5). The sixty-ninth Psalm is echoed in the lines in which the voyager is in peril of the sea:

> I sink in deep mire, where there is no stand-
> ing:
> I am come into deep waters, where the floods
> overflow me.

(69:2)

> Let not the waterflood overflow me, neither
> let
> The deep swallow me up, and let not the pit
> Shut her mouth upon me.

(69:15)

Biblical episodes, literary references, and private images combine to form the hallucinatory landscape and seascape conjured by the hypothetical evangelist, now speaking with the gift of tongues.

The hazards of a quest or journey are introduced by a line which Thomas salvaged from a long, unpublished poem of his (Poem Seventeen in the 1933 Notebook): "For loss of blood I fell where stony hills / Had milk and honey flowing from their cracks." [12] The line is changed to suggest a Biblical setting and literary theme of outcasts and wanderers: Hagar and her child in Genesis and the child's namesake, Ishmael, in *Moby Dick*. The Jonah reference is taken from Father Mapple's sermon in *Moby Dick* and from Jonah 2:1–6. Ishmael, the narrator aboard the *Pequod*, and Jonah, the fugitive aboard the ship bound for Tarshish, encounter whales: both are cast into the sea and both are saved. In the sonnet Ishmael and Jonah are joined by Christ, the third wanderer, who compares himself to Jonah in the prophecy of his resurrection: "For as Jonas was three days and three nights in the whale's belly; so shall the Son of man be three days and three nights in the heart of the earth" (Matthew 12:40). The ship is to Ishmael and the belly of the fish is to Jonah what the tomb is to Christ. All are strangers in that which contains them: Ishmael aboard the *Pequod,* Jonah in the fish, and Christ in the tomb. For each one a three-day period is the crucial time span: the *Pequod* pursues Moby Dick for three days; Jonah is in the fish for three days; Christ is in the tomb three days. All three are "born of the water": Ishmael is nearly sucked into the vortex of the sinking ship but is picked up by the *Rachel;* Jonah is cast into the sea and is rescued by a whale; and Christ is baptized in the Jordan, after which the heavens open.

"For loss of blood I fell on Ishmael's plain" calls to mind at once the two outcasts who were ministered to by angels in the wilderness—Ishmael and Christ. But our attention is shifted to Christ, for it is he who will fall under the weight of the Cross, and it is he who will bleed. "Ishmael's plain" is Thomas's reference to the desert in the Genesis story (21:14–20), and to the sea in *Moby Dick* into which Ishmael falls. Hunger and thirst are the privations of the wanderer in the wilderness who finds milky mushrooms to shelter and sustain him. The image of the mushroom is a combination of pun and mushroom lore. The phrase "under the milky mushrooms" is taken from the Hagar–Ishmael episode: ". . . And the water was spent and she cast the child under one of the shrubs." The Jonah story contributes to that phrase, too: it is under a gourd that Jonah finds shelter from the sun. The mushroom, an anomaly in either Biblical or desert landscape, flourishes in Thomas's own imagination. It is one variation of his many mammary images in his poems.[13] In this sonnet the image suggests the nourishment which sustains the wanderer as embryo, as child, as prophet. Milk mushrooms (*Lactarius subdulcis* and *Lactarius deliciosus*) are edible mushrooms native to the British Isles. Their shape, color, and whitish fluid must have suggested to Thomas shelter, mother's breasts, and milk. But there is another variety, a poisonous species (*Amanita verna*) known popularly as the "destroying angel" because of its death-white color and its deadly effect upon anyone who eats it. When we remember that the angel of the Annunciation, by his prophecy of the Incarnation, dooms Christ to mortality, we can see that he becomes the "destroying angel" as well. And by a leap of imagination we can see that Thomas effects a triple image: that of the unborn child under his mother's heart feeding upon her substance; that of the infant suckling at her breast; and that of the man whose lifeless head rests against his mother's bosom in *Pietà* scenes.

The "climbing sea" may be the amniotic fluid in which the embryo makes its nine-month journey before it is delivered, like Jonah, and cast "upon the dry land." Gestation, Biblical narrative, and Melville's novel are parallel to each other. The "climbing sea" which overwhelms Jonah is described as "The waters compassed me about . . . The deep was round about me; The weeds were wrapped about my head." (Jonah 2:6). In *Moby Dick* we discover the "climbing sea" as an echo of "a combing sea dashed me off . . ." [14] The rescue motif in the next line is an example of Thomas's use of montage effected by fusing two borrowed images from the Bible and Melville. It is "Jonah's Moby" which snatched the drowning pilgrim "by the hair." This is not only rescue according to the lifesaver's manual, but it is also a motif recorded in *Moby Dick* and in the Apochryphal story of Bel and the Dragon. In both instances the hair is seized:

. . . and soon after, Queequeg was seen boldly striking out with one hand, and with the other clutching the long hair of the Indian.[15]

Then the angel of the Lord took him [Habakkuk] by the crown and lifted him up by the hair of his head, and with the blast of his breath set him in Babylon over the den.

(Bel and the Dragon, verse 36)

In the story of Jonah, the whale was the agent of salvation; in the Book of Bel and the Dragon, the prophet Habakkuk came to the help of Daniel; and in *Moby Dick*, it was Queequeg who plunged into the sea to rescue Tashtego. In the sonnet the anonymous pilgrim is saved through the agency of a Biblical–literary whale. Sea imagery and rescue motif suggest Thomas's concept of soteriology: literally, out of the depths the quester is saved through divine agency. Immersion is interpreted by Sandor Ferenczi, in his *Thalassa*, as a return to the uterus, and rescue from the water is explained as "the birth motif or . . . exile to land existence . . ."[16] Nicodemus anticipated Ferenczi by almost two thousand years when he exclaimed in perplexity: "How can man be born when he is old? can he enter a second time into his mother's womb, and be born?" (John 3:4). The journey by water is seen as a rebirth motif by Jung:

Born from the springs, rivers, seas, at death man arrives at the waters of the Styx in order to enter upon the "night journey on the sea." The wish is that the black water of death, with its cold embrace, might be the mother's womb, just as the sea devours the sun, but brings it forth again out of the maternal womb (Jonah motive).[17]

More than three hundred years ago Bishop Lancelot Andrewes made the same observation in a sermon on the Resurrection:

Jonas' hope failed him not; the whale's belly that

65

seemed his tomb, proved his womb or second birth-place. There he was, not as meat in the stomach, but as an embryo in the matrix of his mother. Strange! the whale to be as his mother, to be delivered of him, and bring him forth into the world again.[18] We are cut adrift from syntax and are caught in a vortex of images in boreal and Sargasso seas where neither sextant, quadrant, nor compass is of any use. The lines in this portion of the sonnet are crowded with creatures let loose from heaven, nature, and books. A little lower than the frozen angel are Adam, the bear, the whale, the sirens, and the medusa. Biology, the Bible, and books on arctic travel make it possible for us to identify all the creatures but the frozen angel.

The juxtaposition of a black jellyfish and a frozen angel in polar ice fields is not very far removed from Dali's painting "Persistence of Memory," in which black ants crawl in and out of the works of liquefying watches, a lady views her image in a mirror, and a Portugese man-of-war (a species of medusa) lurks in the lower part of the painting. Perhaps the black medusa and the frozen angel are persistent memories for Thomas: nothing is more persistent in memory than the ice of the Arctic and the tentacles of a medusa. Perhaps it is as futile to attempt to identify the frozen angel as it is to look for the realm of Wallace Stevens' emperor of ice cream in a Rand McNally atlas. The frozen angel may be a mem-ory of fallen innocence or a numb remorse, or it may be a punished rebel, death, obduracy, or a statue, or even a frozen dessert. Sometimes I think of the frozen angel as a child's confection spoiled by a slimy medusa, just as Miss Muffet's curds and whey were made unappetiz-ing by the presence of the spider. I do not know whether this angel is of Thomas's dreams, or recollections, or mystical experience. I do know that the angel is there, fixed and perplexing. And it must be wrestled with.[19]

The landscape in which we see this angel recalls two pilgrims of the dark abyss to whom ice was a metaphor of damnation. The frozen angel is not unlike Dante's Satan, congealed breast-high in ice in the Inferno; and not unlike those souls in Milton's frozen continent, damned to be brought

> From bed of raging fire to starve in ice
> Their soft ethereal warmth, and there to pine
> Immovable, infixed, and frozen round
> Periods of time,—thence hurried back to fire.
>
> (*Paradise Lost*, Book II, ll. 600–603)

We can exclaim with the Voice in the Whirlwind in Job: "Out of whose womb came the ice?" And where, indeed, did the frozen angel come from? There were imaginations before Thomas, capable of conceiving frozen angels. In the Book of Enoch we learn that in the first heaven there are angels who guard the snow and ice:

> And then I looked and saw the treasuries of the snow and ice and the angels who guard their terrible store-places;
>
> (5:1)

Later in his vision Enoch sees another angel:

> And the Lord called up one of the older angels, terrible and menacing, and placed him by me, in appearance white as snow, and his hands like ice, having the appearance of great frost, and he froze my face, because I could not endure the terror of the Lord, just as it is not possible to endure a stove's fire and the sun's heat, and the frost of the air.
>
> (37:1)

I have often wondered whether that angel "of the guarded mount," frozen in stone atop the tower of the abbey church which bears his name, he whom Milton asks to "melt with ruth," might have suggested to Thomas an image of a frozen angel on a hill. And although the frozen angel is not of the company of the Archangel Michael, there is a relevant contrast suggested by the statue on Mont St. Michel, with sword in hand and dragon underfoot, to the other angel atop a polar mound, stung into immobility by a medusa. The bold panoramas of geography in "Lycidas" and in this sonnet, the seascape imagery, the dolphins exhorted to "waft the hapless youth," the whale which "cross-stroked salt Adam," the theme of resurrection in Milton's poem and that of the Nativity in the sonnet may point to "Lycidas" as a possible source of the image of the frozen angel.

The "salt Adam" is more fortunate than Lycidas; like Arion and Jonah he is carried to shore in safety—not a hospitable shore, but one where he will be in cold union with the angel and the medusa. The verb "cross-stroked," which describes a rescue, raises syntactical difficulties. This strange verb is anchored to its object Adam, but where is its subject? Is the subject the "climbing sea," or "Jonah's Moby," or both? And what has happened to the first person singular? Perilous journeys, strange metamorphoses, and portentous events take place in an asyntactical wonderworld. What emerges from these lines is an account of Adam's rescue in a polar setting, recalling scenes from Coleridge's "Ancient Mariner" and Melville's *Moby Dick*.

The Byzantine Adam is now the "salt Adam" because he is a sailor, having made a long journey by water; because he is lustful,[20] and because he and his progeny will be preserved from corruption by that salt which has never lost its savor.[21] I assume Thomas uses the verb "cross-stroked" to describe Moby's motion in bringing Adam to shore. It is Thomas's verbal invention, one of several neologisms which occur in his poems. Donne, in "The Crosse," uses components of this word in reminding us that we are our own crosses: "Swimme, and at every stroake, thou art thy Crosse." Literally, a cross stroke is a line which joins together musical notes of small denomination. Thomas uses the word to describe a swimming stroke or a propulsive movement of the rescuing whale. As a musical term it may be a pun on the ice-cap trio who are not as harmonious as the singing sirens in the last line. Adam, the angel, and the medusa are discords in the universal harmony. "Cross-stroked Adam" is Adam rescued; the price of that rescue is anticipated in the two parts of the verb: the Cross which Christ will bear and the strokes he will receive before Pilate's judgment seat.[22]

I have come to the conclusion that the frozen angel, having fallen from grace, is stung into immobility by an invertebrate organism somewhat lower than the angels in the chain of being. Ice and nettles combine to immobilize the angel in a frigid damnation. "Pin-legged on pole-hills" becomes not only the penal condition of the frozen angel; it also suggests, as does "cross-stroked," the consequences of the angel's fall: the nail-fastened feet of Christ on a hill of cross-poles. The wordplay on pin and pole reminds us that this angel, unlike the mobile angels pirouetting on pinpoints, is fastened to a magnetic point in the North Pole.

The black medusa is one of Thomas's bold triumphs in imagery. Here is an instance of the union effected between poetry and science. In this sonnet the medusa becomes a pelagic Lilith mated to the frozen angel. This union suggests an interesting parallel to a legend in which Lilith becomes the consort of a rebellious angel known as Sammaël, literally, "poison of God." I think the medusa is a marine counterpart of Lilith, Thomas's metaphor of sin. What Thomas attempted to create was, I believe, a compact hell in which the angel, Adam, and the medusa are linked each to the other until a certain event redeems Adam, thaws the angel, and draws out medusa's sting. The hairlike filaments of the medusa, with which it catches and stings its prey into paralysis, relate it to its classical namesake Medusa, whose serpent locks transformed her victims into stone, and to Lilith, who snared her victims by the fatal beauty of her hair.[23]

In presenting his image of the medusa as a metaphor of sin and lust stinging into obduracy and frozen corruption, Thomas observed a mythological convention of

poetic reference. Dante depicts the Medusa as one who
hardens the heart and paralyzes the will. Milton de-
scribes her, in her immobilizing "Gorgonian terror,"
keeping the damned from drinking of Lethe. And Blake
in a variation of the image transforms Hela in *Tiriel* into
a monstrous creature whose ". . . dank hair upright
stood, while snakes infolded round / over madding
brows . . ." [24] Beyond the mythological conceit, how-
ever, Thomas reveals a knowledge of medusae not de-
rived from a classical dictionary. It is not a generally
known fact that the Arctic Ocean is a habitat of me-
dusae. It is possible that Thomas may have found his
information in a text of marine biology. It is more likely,
however, that he found references to polar medusae in
that exhaustive study of the chemistry of Coleridge's
imagination, *The Road to Xanadu*. It is not beyond pos-
sibility that Thomas might have seen the fascinating
notes about marine organisms in that study: his "Bal-
lad of the Long-Legged Bait" is filled with an imagery
reminiscent of "The Ancient Mariner" and *The Road
to Xanadu*.

According to John Livingston Lowes, Coleridge had
read descriptions of medusae in arctic waters recorded
by polar explorers.[25] The current of Coleridge's imagina-
tion swept the plankton from northern seas into tropical
waters, where the Ancient Mariner in his becalmed ship
exclaimed in revulsion:

> The very deep did rot: O Christ!
> That ever this should be!
> Yea, slimy things did crawl with legs
> Upon the slimy sea.

A contemporary of Coleridge, Capt. William Scoresby
(later the Reverend Dr. William Scoresby), marveled in
wonder that

> The Greenland Sea, frozen and extensive as it is,
> teems with life . . . The minute medusae and ani-
> malcules, throughout the Spitzbergen sea, would
> exceed all the powers of the mind to conceive.[26]

His wonder that this teeming life in frozen wastes should be preserved leads him to discover a warmer current underneath the surface, making the seas habitable for these "animalcules." And in an observation that goes beyond oceanography, he concludes that this illustrates "the combined wisdom and goodness of the Lawgiver of these icy regions, as well as of the entire globe." [27] The last statement is not unlike the conclusion of Thomas's sonnet, which binds all nature together at the moment of the Nativity.

More recent findings in marine zoology report specimens of medusa (Cyanea), measuring six feet in diameter, to have been discovered in the Arctic Ocean.[28] Such a medusa could easily sting an angel into immobility for eternity! The color of Thomas's medusa is an attribute transferred, I believe, from a black widow spider. Colors of medusae vary from brown to bright orange or deep red to deep blue or purple.[29] I have not heard of black medusae. Thomas may have allowed his imagination to free him from scientific restriction in choosing a black medusa because of its contrast to the white bear and the polar setting.

The bare whiteness of the arctic landscape is a constant reminder to Adam of what lies between him and the wondrous variety of the lost Garden. In the expulsion of Adam and Eve from Paradise, described in the Pseudepigrapha, we read that "Michael held a rod in his hand, and he touched the waters, which were round about paradise, and they froze hard" (Books of Adam and Eve, 28:3, 4). In this bleak, empty waste of polar seas; in the presence of angelic disobedience, human failure, and invertebrate sin; in a setting of congealed hopelessness, we hear a prophecy. A polar bear, brute force in icy seas, is suddenly possessed of prophetic power to quote Virgil's fourth *Eclogue*, in which the birth of a savior-child is foretold.[30] That a white bear can quote Virgil should not surprise anyone: Balaam's ass was gifted with speech.[31] The white bear's prophecy

71

is followed by an antiphonal response of sirens singing of this strange Nativity from a Sargasso Sea of weeds. All of nature is moved to reveal the miracle that has given it tongue to speak. The same theme appears in an account of the miracles of the Nativity in *The Golden Legend:*

> We know for instance, that it [the Nativity] was revealed to every class of creatures, from the stones, which are at the bottom of the scale of creatures, to the angels, who are at its summit.[32]

Thomas's white bear is a direct descendant of a creature which has received considerable attention from Coleridge, Poe, and Melville. Coleridge, having read about William Barents' encounters with polar bears in *Purchas his Pilgrimage* (Vol. xiii, pp. 36–162) concludes his dreary "Destiny of Nations" with a picture of arctic dreariness:

> And first a landscape rose
> More wild and waste and desolate than where
> The white bear, drifting on a field of ice,
> Howls to her sundered cubs with piteous rage
> And savage agony.[33]

Melville has much to say about the polar bear and its whiteness in *Moby Dick.* He had read Coleridge and, very likely, Poe's *Narrative of A. Gordon Pym,* in which there are two striking passages about whiteness and a terrifying white bear. Melville's famous chapter on the whiteness of the whale contains a lengthy footnote on the polar bear:

> With reference to the Polar bear, it may possibly be urged by him who would fain go still deeper into this matter, that it is not the whiteness, separately regarded, which heightens the intolerable hideousness of that brute; for, analysed, that heightened hideousness, it might be said, only arises from the circumstance, that the irresponsible ferociousness of the creature stands invested in the fleece of celestial innocence and love; and hence,

by bringing together two such opposite emotions in our minds, the Polar bear frightens us with so unnatural a contrast. But even assuming all this to be true; yet, were it not for the whiteness, you would not have that intensified terror.[34]

Thomas annihilates distance in his swift movement from the Arctic Ocean to the Sargasso Sea where the sirens, instead of luring to destruction with their irresistible voices, become sibyls chanting a new hope amid the strands of "our lady's sea-straw." Here is an instance of Thomas's cunning montage in effecting a shift from sea to manger. "Our lady's sea-straw" is Thomas's variation of Our Lady's bedstraw (*Galium verbum*), or yellow bedstraw. The plant takes its popular name from a charming Nativity legend that it was one of the herbs in the straw upon which Mary rested in the stable.[35]

We travel a long distance in this sonnet from Hollywood to Holy Land, pausing to watch card tricks and wonder at miracles. There are moments when we feel we are with Doughty in Arabia as we falter on Ishmael's plain. And there are moments when we feel we are in the ice fields with Nansen or Shackleton. Botany and zoology, geography and theology, the Bible and classical mythology combine in this sonnet to tempt the reader into an abjuration of poetic faith.[36] But if the reader can suspend his disbelief long enough to share Tertullian's credo that one believes because it is absurd, then he will find emerging from the apparent absurdity of this sonnet a statement of faith. The statement is dragged, submerged, obscured: but finally it becomes clear. Between Annunciation and Nativity there is biology. The natural is as miraculous as the supernatural: gestation is a form of incarnation. We are witness to Thomas's awe, mortal fear, defensive puns, and gentle wonder as he enters this sonnet with a noisy bang and leaves it in quiet sibilants.

6

Sonnet VI

And the earth was without form and void—and darkness
was upon the face of the deep. And the spirit of God moved
upon the face of the waters. And God said, Let there be
light: and there was light.

Genesis 1:2, 3

In the beginning was the Word . . .

John 1:1

IN THE SIXTH SONNET Thomas reworks the opening
verses of Genesis and the Fourth Gospel to produce an
effect of a cosmic orgy. The imagery is seismic and
surgical. From an inchoate, wet vastness the Logos in
its parturition erupts into a cosmos. Simultaneously
there is a genesis of mutilated shape from primal ooze.
The long night of uncreated void is over, and the amor-
phousness of chaos is at an end. The scenes recall the
subterranean furnaces and mountainous seas of Blake's
prophetic books, the obscene noises of Goethe's Wal-
purgis Night scene, and the cabalistic language of the
Zohar.[1]
That Thomas was familiar with Blake's poems and
Goethe's *Faust* I have no doubt. Whether Thomas had
ever looked at a translation of the *Zohar*, that dark-
lanterned brilliance, I do not know. There was one
available to him, published in England in 1932. It is
more likely that Thomas, like Yeats, was attracted to

the numerous books of esoterica written by Arthur E. Waite about such subjects as alchemy, demonology, angelology, Tarot cards, magic, and the *Cabala*. The arcane systems, the hierarchies of emanations, the fantastic cosmologies, and the intricate organization of chaos described in Waite's *The Doctrine and Literature of the Kabalah* appealed to the imagination of Yeats; I think it might have appealed to the imagination of Thomas, too. In 1930 Denis Saurat's *Literature and the Occult Tradition* was published in England. At least one-third of the work is devoted to the *Cabala* and the *Zohar;* part of the work deals with Blake's interest in cabalistic lore. Perhaps Thomas was attracted to this work because of its comments on Blake and the *Cabala*.[2] This is all conjecture. Not conjectural, however, is the evidence in the sixth sonnet of the theme of God's mystical division of his own substance into cosmos and man. This is a theme to which Saurat devotes considerable comment. The first section of the *Zohar*, which is a commentary on Genesis 1:1–6, is filled with an imagery that suggests an interesting parallel to the sonnet sequence.[3]

The similarity between the *Zohar* and this sonnet consists largely in the language. The language in the *Zohar*, in its anagogical interpretation of Genesis, is mystical and sexual. The language in the sonnet describing Genesis (really catagenesis) is equally mystical and sexual, differing only in its irony and irreverence. There are other similarities even more distinct. Thomas makes much of vowels in his reference to the divine utterance which precedes light. The *Zohar*, contradicting the meaning of its name, speaks obscurely of God sowing a sacred seed which was to generate itself for the benefit of the universe. The seed consists of letters which, with vowel points (vowel sounds above or below consonants), combined to form the Voice. The alphabet is endowed with numerical value, mystical significance, and procreative power. The combination of the vowels

75

symbolizes a sexual union. Thus the word *Yehi* (let there be) signifies a union of the Father and Mother, symbolized by the letters *Yod He* (Y, H), making creation possible. The anagogical never departs too far from the biological in the *Zohar*.

The first four lines of the sonnet are a parody of the Creation. The power of the Word and light, as generative and formative forces in Genesis, is regarded with derisiveness and contempt. The Word becomes the "oyster vowel," and the light is nothing more than a "wick of words." The Creator of the primordial wonder is described in comic strip language ("cartoon of slashes") brooding over waters in a pitted, volcanic landscape ("tide-traced crater"). Here is God, a tallow-eyed, archcabalist, sitting over a book of water, studying far into uncreated night. "Cartoon" may be taken in its original meaning: a design drawn on pasteboard to serve as a model for a work of art. God is a "tallow-eyed" planner because he burns the midnight candle over his cartoon, arranging the secret words which will bring order out of chaos. The volcanic crater image, "By lava's light," is a pun suggesting the flow of light from Yahweh, the old volcanic deity. "The oyster vowels" are unuttered words: closed oysters at the bottom of the shoreless sea are a metaphor of silence. And it is God who dredges them up, splits them open, and finds the pearls, the vowels of oysters. Through his omnipotence he is able to split the silence with his Word: "Let there be light." And the great miracle is wrought as the sea silence is burned on a wick of words. "In the beginning was the Word": and before the power of the Word, which is here a lighted wick, the dark waters of primeval silence recede.

The imagery in the rest of the sonnet is a fusion of marine biology, Greek mythology, literary analogues, and cabalistic legend. "Medusa's scripture" is primeval, as old as the "book of water," reminding one of a Blake illustration called *Hecate*, in which he depicts Vala

(*The Four Zoas*) as an incarnation of the female will, with the serpentine book of good and evil open at her feet.[4] The scriptures of medusa are perhaps Thomas's analogue to Genesis. The emphasis on creation and procreation in this sonnet recalls Denis Saurat's description, in his *Literature and the Occult Tradition,* of the androgynous nature of God as a process of division and reconstitution:

> The Demiurge creates the world or becomes the world by an act which . . . is a cosmic parallel to the sexual act. In its extreme expression we find the hermaphrodite God, who divides himself and whose parts fecundate each other; hence the theme of divine incest.[5]

The phenomenon of the reproduction of a polyp such as a fresh-water hydra offers a distinct biological parallel to the legends of divine procreation cited by Saurat —particularly distinct since the result of the process is a medusa.[6]

The presence of the medusa in this sonnet offers us another opportunity to examine the process of Thomas's image making. Thomas's imagination, always an ingenious alembic, could have produced lamiae, melusinae, and Empusae for the occasion; but like Goethe in his classical Walpurgis Night scene, Thomas was restrained and selective.[7] The medusa served his purpose well. To marine biologists the medusa is "a beautiful little jelly-fish," [8] but to Thomas it is a metaphor of primal sexuality, sin, and the eternally dangerous female. The medusa was chosen as metaphor because its habitat is water, and water is the fundamental element in Genesis. This organism, as I have indicated in the previous chapter, is the biological namesake of the mythological Medusa with whom it shares its lethal paralytic power. Its long hairlike filaments have the same effect as the Medusa's serpentine locks. The outer filaments of the medusa are sticky, enabling it to entangle its prey. At the same time, its inner filaments,

77

the nematocysts, inject a paralytic drug into its victim.[9] The predatory habits of this hydrozoa and the sex of the Gorgonian Medusa endow Thomas's jellyfish with its female attributes. Later in the sonnet the medusa undergoes a variety of transformations into a witch, a stinging siren, and a nettlefish—all manifestations of the female will.

The imagery of marine life seems to have fascinated Thomas, a fascination shared by other poets. In his story of Hermaphroditus and Salmacis, Ovid describes a polypus (from which the medusa is an evolved form) as a symbol of female absorption in whose tentacles male identity is crushed.[10] Blake, in a similar image, illustrating the procreative and annihilating quality of the female will, speaks of

> . . . a vast Polypus
> Of living Fibres down into the Sea of Time
>   and growing
> A self-devouring monstrous Human Death
>   Twenty-seven fold,
> Within sit Five Females and the nameless
>   shadowy Mother
> Spinning it from their bowels with songs of
>   amorous delight
> And melting cadences that lure the Sleepers
>   of Beulah down
> The River Storge (which is Arnon) into the
>   Dead Sea.[11]

Goethe's classical Walpurgis Night (Part II) suggests an oceanic kinship with this sonnet in its scenes crowded with sirens, Dorides, and Phorkyads. Goethe attempted to achieve the ideal ugliness in this part of his poem; Thomas, not to be outdone, achieves an equal ideal of the horrible and the repulsive. His description of mating, surgery, and birth in obstetrical imagery suggests a maternity hospital and operating room at the bottom of a Sargasso Sea, with a variety of jellyfish and sirens as nurses and midwives.

The turbulent, cataclysmic imagery describing the creation of the universe ("split . . . vowels / burned sea silence") changes to a violent surgical imagery ("pluck . . . eye / lop . . . tongue"). The creative power of God is in his eye (light) and in his tongue (the Word), for with this power he banished darkness and filled the void. Is God creating of his own substance the Son to be offered up to the world? Implied in the Creation is the necessary sacrifice which, in the language of Blake, might be described as "the cruelties of holiness." [12] The light of the world must be put out, and the Word made flesh must be silenced so that by a divine paradox men might be made to see and to hear.

The "pin-hilled nettle" is a description of a nettle-fish, another name for the stinging jellyfish or medusa. As a compressed metaphor "pin-hilled nettle" suggests death, the sting of sin. In this synonym for jellyfish there is a triple reference to the nails (pin), mount (hill), and crown of thorns (nettle) of the Crucifixion. The word "pin-hilled" itself is derived from a transposition of the components of "pole-hills" and "pin-legged" in the previous sonnet.

The imagery in the next four lines is fashioned out of wordplay, Scripture, and classical mythology. "Sea-eye" and "fork tongue" are attributes of the medusa, now called "the stinging siren." The long tentacles radiating from the center suggest an eye with long lashes; the serpents of the Medusa are the source of the "fork tongue." Lopped tongue and plucked sea-eye are themes in two of Ovid's tales from the *Metamorphoses:* the description in Book VI of Philomela's severed tongue, twitching and writhing convulsively as if it were the tail of a mutilated snake; and the account in Book IV of the theft, by Perseus, of the single eye shared among the three Graeae, daughters of Phorcys, a sea deity. The connection between eye and serpent becomes even more apparent when we remember that it was with the stolen eye that Perseus was able to find the home of the Gorgons, where he killed the Medusa.

Mythology yields to morality when we hear an echo of Milton and Scripture in the imperatives of "lop . . . tongue" and "pluck . . . eye." As sources of temptation the eye and the tongue are dangerous organs. Thus Milton:

> . . . fair female troop . . .
> Bred only and completed to the taste
> Of lustful appetence, to sing, to dance,
> To dress, and troll the tongue, and roll the
>   eye.

(Paradise Lost, Book XI, ll. 610–616)

It is the "minstrel tongue" of the singing sirens which lures the victim within range of the eye of the "stinging siren." Hence the siren's eye is plucked out and the minstrel tongue is lopped off by "old cock from nowheres," the mysterious autogenetic force of the first sonnet. Thomas translates Biblical verse into "medusa's scripture" by amending to his own purpose the verse "And if thy right eye offend thee, pluck it out . . . And if thy right hand offend thee, cut it off" (Matthew 5:29–30).

The "I" in the ninth line who blew tallow is the omnipresent spectator, the poet, or primordial chronicler of the events in these sonnets. He is a protean, ambiguous, formidable adversary of syntax. He is also witness, at the midnight hour, to fearful and strange conjurings. One has the feeling that the setting in the octave is a subcosmic, oceanic cave where a profane ritual is performed by sirens, Adam, the animated playing card (his cardboard consort), and a chorus of bagpipe-breasted ladies. The bagpipe recalls at once two witches' sabbaths: one in "Tam O'Shanter," where the devil himself plays the pipes for the assembly of witches; and the other on the Blocksberg in the Walpurgis Night scene in *Faust*, Part I.[13] We are witness to a nativity: the old Adam has already been created out of tallow, the animal fats of midnight. And the second Adam, made of wax (not tallow), is about to be born. The distinction between wax and tallow is important because the beeswax of which sacramental candles are molded is considered "a pure and indestructible substance, mysteriously made." [14] The beeswax candle came early to be regarded as a symbol of the flesh of Christ.

The contrast between the nativities in the fifth and sixth sonnets is distinct. In Thomas's Christology there are two nativities: the patrogenesis and the parthenogenesis of the Son.[15] The wax's tower is Thomas's phallic metaphor of God as a burning candle whose dripping wax forms manwax.[16] Whether he knew it or not, Thomas shared his candle image with St. Augustine, Vincent of Beauvais, Langland, and the anonymous author of the Candlemas mystery play. The candle or taper in medieval theology and allegory served as a homely symbol of the Trinity: the wax, wick, and flame represented the humanity, soul, and godhead of Christ. Or as the learned saw it: *ignis, calor, splendor;* fire, heat, and light. The moral symbolists endowed each part of the candle with an attribute of Christ: the wick, his humility; the wax, his obedience; the flame, his love. Judging from the rate of combustion in this sonnet, Thomas burns the candle at both ends. There is much heat, little light, a strong odor of burned tallow, and no fragrance of beeswax. There is, instead, a suggestion of lubricity, not love; of greasy stain, not anointing; of ritual orgy, not the rite of Purification (Candlemas).

The extinction of the candle and the bloody gauze are a reminder of the Tenebrae services of Holy Week, when, one by one, fourteen candles are snuffed out; the fifteenth candle, representing Christ, is hidden ("buried") under the Epistle corner of the altar. The church is darkened in re-enactment of the extinction of the light of the world. After a Paternoster, a psalm (the 50th), and a prayer are said in the darkness, a noise is made by clapping the choir books to symbolize the convulsion of nature at the Crucifixion. The hidden candle,

81

still lit, is then replaced, and all depart. When I consider the sequence of episodes in the sixth sonnet, I am struck by its close resemblance to the Tenebrae service. The sonnet begins with the creation of light; it ends with the extinction of the "manwax." The Tenebrae service begins in light and concludes in darkness, followed by the restoration, however, of the hidden lighted candle. The sonnet ends with the noise of a cosmic orgy; the Tenebrae service concludes with a clapping of books to signify the cosmic revulsion at the Crucifixion. And lastly, in the Tenebrae service, the lighted candle is removed from its hiding place to signify the deathlessness of Christ; in the sonnet, however, the candle flame is extinguished by the breath of the bagpipe-breasted ladies.

The sirens' song is not a song of jubilation or wonder; it is the music of lust ("When the salt was singing") which introduces the old Adam astride his witch. Adam is "time's joker," the extra card in the deck. Not only is he a joker in the slang sense of "fellow" or "creature"; he is also the card of special value—God's trump card, a triumph of creation. The joker is also the card which runs wild in the deck. And there he is astride a witch of cardboard, the medusa transformed into a playing-card Lilith.

The legend of Lilith fascinated the cabalists. Her origin is probably Babylonian, and in Semitic demonology she appears as a powerful creature whose maleficent presence and awful curses have inspired many a deprecatory ritual. It is in Talmudic legends, cabalistic lore, Apocryphal literature, and folklore that Lilith exists in her full dark identity with terrifying potency.[17] Certain Rabbinical writings describe Lilith as having been created with Adam, joined back to back. Perpetual quarreling made it necessary for God to separate them. The legend closest to this sonnet describes Lilith as the "wife of him who rode upon her back, and this was Sammaël the death-angel."[18] Adam astride his witch of cardboard imitates Sammaël. Lilith is sometimes described as an amphibious demon; [19] in this sonnet her cardboard counterpart manages to stay afloat with Adam astride her. One is tempted to trace the ancestry of the bagpipe-breasted ladies in the deadweed to Lilith, who, legend tells us, was the mother of a night brood of evil spirits engendered by Adam.[20]

Adam's union with his cardboard consort in this sonnet endows him with a double facility of prophecy and curse. The meaning of "spelt out the seven seas, an evil index," is twofold. "Spelt out" is an archaic term for prognosticate, and "the seven seas" are the collective term for the world, the seven land masses separated by the seven seas.[21] The "evil index" is "medusa's scripture" or Lilith's list of curses.[22] Adam is prophetic in foretelling the innumerable woes of mankind. "Spelt out the seven seas, an evil index" may mean Adam's malediction upon each sea, and therefore upon the whole world. The curses, then, become an index or list of evils in medusa's (or Lilith's) scripture.

It is the malign power that Lilith has over women in labor and over infants that makes her presence in this sonnet so baleful. She and her retinue of ˄lemons cause women pain in travail, and hover over a woman in labor to snatch the child away. Women in childbirth wear amulets to ward off her powerful spell, and mothers hang amulets around the necks of their newborn infants to protect them from Lilith.[23] The significance of Adam's evil index becomes apparent in the bloody imagery of mutilation and extinction in the last two lines when the bagpipe-breasted ladies, night-hag midwives, attend the delivery of one of Adam's descendants.[24] There is no singing from Our Lady's sea-straw; instead there is the silent blowing out of blood gauze through manwax. A surgical image and an extinguished candle conclude this sonnet, anticipating the bloody linen cloth girding the loins of Christ, dead against a darkened sky at the ninth hour.[25] It is difficult at this moment in the poem to believe with John of Revelation (22:5) that "there shall be no night there and they need no candle." The sonnet ends, as it begins, in the darkness and silence that were before Creation: the light of the world gone out, the Word stilled.

7

Sonnet VII

Our Father who art in heaven . . .
                        Matthew 6:9

Always pray to a tree, said the gardener,
thinking of Calvary and Eden.
                        Dylan Thomas, "The Tree"

AFTER THE COSMIC ERUPTION and Adam's noisy lechery
in the medusa-crowded sea, after the mutilation of eye
and tongue, after the blood gauze and deadweed, there
is a very brief calm in the turbulence of the poem. The
calm is perfectly timed, for it comes between the primal
birth in the sixth sonnet and the Crucifixion in the
eighth.

Here, as in all the sonnets of this sequence, the sestet
precedes the octave, but with this difference: the event
in the eight lines below produces the effect in the six
lines above. The sestet is composed mainly of vegeta-
tion imagery: rice grain, leaves, woods, trees, root; the
element is the earth. In the octave the element in the
first four lines is water, where the shapeless thing born
and mutilated in the sixth sonnet, now described as
a sponge, is suckled at the musical teats of the bagpipe-
breasted ladies. The fifth line contains a transition from
the scene of primordial maternal figures to the Nativity
scene in Bethlehem. The fourth repetition of "time"

concludes the sonnet in a couplet describing the ineluctable effect of time on nature and man.

The first line does not exhort to prayer; it is the first of two urgent imperatives. The commands are given by an invisible narrator, perhaps the poet himself. The first imperative with its adverb "now" implies the immediate necessity of creating a talisman in the form of a rice grain, not unlike those medallions and miniature coins upon which the Lord's Prayer is inscribed. The line also suggests the parable of the grain of mustard seed "which a man took, and cast into his garden; and it grew, and waxed a great tree" (Luke 13:19).

The inscribed rice grain, like the mustard seed, has now sprouted into a many-leaved Bible made of all the trees in the world; it is the multiplication of the Word into many words. "Written woods" is a play on written words or printed pulp. It is this book or Bible which Thomas commands to be stripped to the tree. The verb "strip" seems to suggest a separative genitive, as in "strip the leaves or bark *from* this tree." Does Thomas ask that the Tree of Knowledge be stripped of its fruit, or does he refer to the bark-stripped rood, or does he mean Christ, stripped of his garments? But the phrase is "strip *to* this tree"; and it is the preposition which gives "strip" a special meaning in the context of Thomas's imagery of books. "Strip" is a bookbinding term, and therefore the sense of the line is: "bind these leaves to this tree." In bookbinding "strip" is the process of affixing strips of muslin or book cloth to the edges of pads or over the fold of a cover or insert to hold the pages and cover of the book together. "Strip" is also a logger's term for marking a particular tree for cutting: the tree out of which the Cross is to be hewn. And lastly, "strip" may also mean "bind." Thomas asks that the Bible be stripped or bound to the tree as a posted warning containing an alpha-omega history, literally the ABC or christcross-row of creation and destruction. The same thought is contained in a fifteenth-century acrostic called *An Alphabetical Devotion to the Cross* which records the Passion of Christ:

> Here begynneth the A.B.C. of devocion
> ✠ Of ihu criste be euer oure spede,
> And kepe us from perel of synnes and payne!
> Blessid be that lorde that on the crosse dide blede,
> Crist, god and man, that for us was slayne,
> Dede he was and rose up agayne.
> Ever helpe us, crosse, with hym to a-ryse
> Ffro deeth to lyve and synne to dispise! [1]

In an earlier poem Thomas used the same image of the hornbook alphabet: "He had by heart the Christ-cross-row of death." [2] The christcross-row was marked by a cross at the beginning and at the end of the alphabet. There is a suggestion of the terminal letters in the "rocking alphabet," the tree of alpha and omega swaying in the wind. The tree in the Garden and the tree on Golgotha are "genesis in the root" sprouting into the Word. Donne, in the "Hymne to God my God, in my sickness," speaks of these two trees in one:

> We think that Paradise and Calvary
> Christs Cross and Adams tree stood in one place

The "book of water" has now changed into a book of trees. [3] It is Thomas's way of contracting Genesis into two essential episodes: out of chaos the Garden is formed, and out of the tree of disobedience grows the tree of submission. The "one light's language" is a synonym for both Testaments: the light which was simultaneous with the first imperative when the uttered words became created light; and the Word which John in the Fourth Gospel describes as the "true light" (1:9).

The "scarecrow word" reminds us that the Word made flesh looked like a scarecrow on the Cross, frightening away those of little faith, Peter in particular. I believe it is to Peter that the stern imprecation "Doom on deniers at the wind-turned statement" refers. The wind-turned statement is a weathercock image suggesting (1) Peter's turning whichever way the wind blew, (2) the cockcrow at the third denial, and (3) his little faith when the wind blew up in a storm over the Sea of Galilee (Matthew 14:24–32).

The shift to the octave is abrupt. There seems to be neither transitional imagery nor extended theme to bridge the division between the two parts of the sonnet. But the division is only apparent: the sestet is bound to the octave by the events described in each. First we learn of several episodes in the ministry of Jesus: the Sermon on the Mount, the spread of the Gospel, the denial of Christ by Peter, the Crucifixion. In the second part of the sonnet we learn of the ontogeny of the Word as it moves from the phase of "sponge" in the sea to the form of a baby born in Bethlehem.

The exhortation to stamp the Lord's Prayer on a grain of rice has two effects: it prepares us for the Crucifixion in the next sonnet, and it has an effect on the sirens lurking in the sixth sonnet. Here the sirens are transformed into beneficent wet nurses offering lullaby and nourishment. The sirens' song is always the song of death, but their tune now is not without tenderness.[4] The bagpipe-breasted ladies are primal mothers, the timeless genetrices whom Goethe invokes with such awe as "Die Mütter! Die Mütter!" in *Faust* (Part II, Act I, l. 182).

The mythological sirens and their lyres are transformed by Thomas into bagpipe-breasted "scaled sea-sawers" who nourish the suckling sponge with music and milk. The metamorphosis of the classical sirens with their lyres into "scaled sea-sawers" is effected by a pun. The pun is an involved series of variations on *scales* and *seesaw*. The marine creatures are "scaled" because they are musical and because they have fish scales. They are "sea-sawers" because formerly they were the "sirens singing from our lady's sea-straw," and they seesaw with the rise and fall of the waves.

"Time's tune" ("the tune of time"—Hamlet V, 2, 198)
is the song of the necessary and destined agony of
which the scaled sea-sawers sing long in advance of the
Nativity. Theirs is a song from the depths of the sea
mortally different from the song of the angels on high.
The sponge into which the ladies fix their teats of music
is the amorphous substance in the sea "from the world
beginning" which will eventually take on human shape
and form. The sponge is the pelagic avatar of Christ,
long before his birth is heralded in the sky in the form
of a bright star; it is a surgical absorbent in ready sup-
ply in delivery and operating rooms (recalling us to
Nativity and Crucifixion); and it is one of the instru-
ments of the Passion, the sponge dipped in hyssop and
given Christ.

As the second Adam in embryo, the sponge is a per-
sonification of redemption. The relative pronoun "who"
in the ninth line ("who sucks the bell-voiced Adam out
of magic") refers to the sponge; a synthesis of prenatal
biology and primal soteriology triumph over the am-
biguity of syntax. This is the last time Adam appears in
the sequence. His presence is by now a familiar one,
his existence a necessary terminal in the long journey of
this poem. Adam has appeared in every sonnet so far
except in the fourth; his absence in the last three sonnets
is significant: redemption makes him superfluous.

The sponge sucks out of magic its divinity, out of
time its mortality, and out of milk its humanity: a gen-
erative force emerges as love. We have here the state-
ment that Christ as second Adam becomes the Re-
deemer who draws up ("sucks out") the rutting Adam,
the bell-voiced Adam ("bell" is the sound of a buck in
rutting time) from the seven seas in which we last saw
him, astride his cardboard witch. The essential distinc-
tion between these two Adams is made clear in their
genesis: Adam is born of the Word breathed into dust;
Christ is born of the Word breathed into flesh.

The great adversary now is Time, which tracks its
prey. Thomas combines the language of the hunt

("track"), of the movies (sound track), and of archaeology ("handprint" is the preserved print of a hand on rocks found in prehistoric caves) to observe that time leaves its traces on all creation: on the rose which it withers, on the icicle which it melts, on the cloud which it dissolves, and on man whom it overcomes. Once the "walking word" leaves the "bald pavilions," its home in the heavenly mansions, time begins to stalk it. "The pavilion of heaven is bare," says Shelley in "The Cloud." The Word, as bare as the heavenly pavilion, is swaddled in its earthly home, "the house of bread," the literal translation of Bethlehem from the Hebrew.

That Thomas was interested in the sermons of the seventeenth century is evident in the title of one of his later poems, "Deaths and Entrances," taken from Donne's sermon "Death's Duell." How familiar he was with the great sermons of Lancelot Andrewes on the Nativity, Passion, and Resurrection it is difficult to say. There are, in this sonnet, frequent parallels to the elaborate conceits and distinct vocabulary which characterize the sermons of the Bishop of Winchester. Twice in this sequence, once in the fourth and once again in this sonnet, Thomas refers to Bethlehem as the "bread-sided field" and "house of bread." Lancelot Andrewes devotes almost an entire Nativity sermon (Christmas Day, 1615) to the meaning of Bethlehem, moving from a literal translation to theological wordplay. The sermon is based on a text from Micah 5:2, which predicts the birth of a Messiah in Bethlehem, thus giving Andrewes an opportunity to construct a sustained conceit which not only describes the birthplace of Christ but also the nourishing efficacy of the Eucharist:

1. . . . the very name of Bethlehem, that is "the house of bread." For He that was born there was "Bread."
2. *Beth* is a house, *lehem* bread . . .
3. Never take Him without bread, His house is the house of bread inasmuch as He Himself is

90

Bread; that in the house or out of it—where-
soever He is, there is Bethlehem. There can no
bread want.

4. Bethlehem, the house of bread, is His house.

5. And in this respect it may well be said, Bethle-
hem was never Bethlehem right, had never the
name truly till this day this birth, this Bread
was born and brought forth there. Before it was
the house of bread, but of the bread that perish-
eth; but then of the "Bread that endureth to
everlasting life."

6. . . . and where that Bread is, there is Bethle-
hem ever.[5]

Andrewes, like Thomas, speaks of pavilions. In his
Christmas sermon of 1611 he speaks of the Word as
having not only taken a house, the flesh, but "pitched
a pavilion in us." And once again, in describing the In-
carnation in a military figure of speech, Andrewes says:
"He, as this day, came into the camp, set up His pavilion
among us."

The pavilions which the Word left and Bethlehem to
which the incarnate Word came are not the only two
images which Andrewes and Thomas share. The alpha-
bet and book images in Thomas's sonnet have their
metaphorical counterparts in Andrewes:

In the very letters, He taketh to Him the name of
"Alpha" the Author, and again of "Omega," the
Finisher of the alphabet.[6]

The extended image of Christ as a book of love (which
Thomas describes as the "scarecrow word") is devel-
oped by Andrewes in an excruciatingly painful conceit:

For sure, if ever aught were truly said of our Sav-
iour, this was: that being spread and laid wide
open on the cross, He is *Liber charitatis* [the book
of love], wherin he that runneth by may read,
Sic dilexit [thus he loved], and *Propter nimiam
charitatem* [Because of love beyond measure], and
Ecce quantum charitatem [Behold such great

love]; love all over, from one end to the other. Every stripe as a letter, every nail as a capital letter. His *livores* [bruises] as black letters, His bleeding wounds as so many rubrics, to show upon record his love toward us.[7]

The image of the tree and embryo in the seventh sonnet is parallel to the extended metaphors in Andrewes's sermons. In his sermon on the Resurrection (March 27, 1608) we find:

Christ is risen, that concerneth us alike. "The head" is got above the water, "the root" has received life and sap, "the first fruits" are lift up and consecrate; we no less than they, as His members, His branches, His field, recover to this hope.[8]

And in another sermon there is a fusion of the metaphors of tree and embryo, including a reference to the corruptive Adam—Thomas's "bell-voiced Adam." The imagery reminds one not only of Dylan Thomas but of Pavel Tschelitchew. Andrewes explains why it was necessary for Christ to be conceived of woman:

For our conception being the root as it were, the very groundsill of our nature; that He might go to the root and repair our nature from the very foundation, thither He went; that what had been there defiled and decayed by the first Adam, might by the Second be cleansed and set aright again . . . He was not idle all the time He was an embryo —all the nine months He was in the womb; but then and there He even eat out the core of corruption that cleft to our nature and us . . .[9]

And, finally, in the music of Thomas's "scaled seasawers" with "teats of music" we may hear the echo of Andrewes's sermon based on Luke 2:14 (Christmas, 1619): "Glory to God in the highest. . . ." Thomas's music comes from below, from a chorus of ondines or nereids; or, as Lancelot Andrewes says: "Here below it is, as it were the cellar or vault of the world." Andrewes,

92

in tune with the infinite, divides the angelic anthem into three parts:

> To God glory, to earth peace, to men . . . good-will. . . .

> But if, as it is most proper, we consider the parts as in a song, the three will agree with the scale in music. . . .
> Time in music is much. And if we will keep time with the Angels, do it when they do it [sing *Gloria in excelsis*]—this day they did it; and what fitter time to sing it than the day it was first sung, the day of the first singing of it . . . ? [10]

But Thomas's music is not sung in concert with the angels; the tune of time which "my ladies lend their heartbreak" is the lament of nature moved to compassion in the same way that the white bear, in its wonder at the prodigious event of the Nativity, was moved to quote Virgil. That tune and heartbreak may be heard in the words of Simeon as he tells Mary: "Your own soul shall have a sword to pierce it" (Luke 2:35). We are now prepared to see the fulfillment of that prophecy in "God's Mary in her grief" in the eighth sonnet.

8

Sonnet VIII

My God, my God, why hast thou forsaken me?
                              Matthew 27:46

Stabat Mater dolorosa
Juxta Crucem lacrimosa
Dum pendebat Filius.
                    Jacopone da Todi

THIS IS THE CLIMAX of the poem. The first seven sonnets
move toward this mountain in a steady ascent. The
eighth sonnet marks the religious and dramatic division
in the sequence. The first seven sonnets, like the seven
days in Genesis, mark the old dispensation; the last
three sonnets, like the last three days of the Passion,
mark the new dispensation with their themes of Cruci-
fixion, burial, and Resurrection. It is here that Thomas
achieves the fearful symmetry of Calvary: the Cross it-
self; Christ crucified between two thieves; the Son sus-
pended between the Father in Heaven and the mother
at the foot of the Cross; the nailed Mediator between
Heaven and earth, mingling both substances in him-
self.

   In its narrative content the eighth sonnet follows the
Gospel accounts of the Passion closely. In mood and
tone the sonnet suggests a *Stabat Mater* hymn or a
medieval *planctus*. In its brutal imagery the sonnet re-
calls the instruments of the Passion; and in its baroque

conceits it resembles the work of the metaphysical poets, especially Donne and Crashaw. Of the ten sonnets this is the simplest, the least obscure, and the most moving.

The clinical image of Christ as a raw nerve dipped in vinegar emphasizes the bitterness and pain of his great humiliation. And it leaves one with an astringent sense of time—time contracted and shrunken into one thin nerve; a quivering, crucial moment in history. As a symbol of the Passion the nerve in vinegar recalls the passage in Matthew 27:48: "And straightway one of them ran, and took a sponge, and filled it with vinegar, and put it on a reed, and gave him to drink." The "gallow grave" is at once Golgotha and the tomb donated by Joseph of Arimathea. The grave is "tarred with blood," suggesting not only black clots of gore but implying a lynching as well. The bloody tears Christ weeps are tears of thorns which pierce his eyes as the crown of thorns pierces his brow. This last image of tears, an instance of a metaphysical conceit, is repeated in the sixth line.

It is difficult at times to determine who the speaker is in the sonnet. The "Jack Christ," for example, is confusing because it sounds like direct address.[1] But Thomas has mixed pronouns and shifted tenses before; and the only conclusion I can draw is that his identification with Christ in this sonnet is complete. We have here a restatement of St. Paul's "I am crucified with Christ: nevertheless I live . . ." (Galatians 2:20). The action of the sonnet is set in the past, but Christ speaks in the historical present and the simple past tense. In the seventh line it is Thomas who speaks for a moment, in the role of guide, to point out the place of the Crucifixion; but, before the line is ended, Christ speaks again.

The best possible way for the reader to understand the many voices in this sonnet is to imagine Thomas as a photographer with recording equipment witnessing the Crucifixion from several angles at the same time that he is recording the thoughts of the chief participants in the drama. An examination of Donne's sonnet "Annunciation" will make clear what Thomas has attempted to achieve in the multiple voices heard in the eighth sonnet. Donne marvels at the many varieties of family relationship brought about by the Incarnation:

> Ere by the spheares time was created, thou
> Wast in his minde, who is thy Sonne, and
>   Brother;
> Whom thou conceiv'st, conceiv'd; yea thou
>   art now
> Thy Makers maker, and thy Fathers mother;

In the unspoken grief given voice by Thomas, we know of the mother's anguish, the Son's agony, God's thought, and the spectator's feeling. So, too, in Jacopone da Todi's "Stabat Mater dolorosa" we learn, through the compassion of the poet, Mary's grief and Christ's humiliation.[2]

As he looks down upon those at the foot of the Cross, Christ remembers that he suffers for the whole world —the world is his wound;[3] and then he beholds his mother, "God's Mary in her grief," bowed down by her great sorrow. He sees her "bent like three trees," a striking image of empathy; she is bent in pain for the three who are crucified. And she is bent like "three trees" because there are three Maries at the Crucifixion. There she stands at the foot of the Cross, the "long wound's woman," her heart torn by the agony of the long wound. "Bird-papped through her shift" describes the thin, slight mother and recalls the earlier "pelican of circles" at which Christ was suckled. "Bird-papped" is derived, probably, from "Blessed be the paps which Thou hast sucked" (Luke 11:27). And as she weeps, her tears fall like pindrops, so piercing is this sight to her eyes. This last image recalls Crashaw's poem on a similar theme, the "Sancta Maria Dolorum":

I

> In shade of Death's sad Tree
>   Stood doleful she.
> Ah she! now by none other

96

Name to be known, alas, but Sorrow's Mother.
   Before her eyes
Her's and the whole World's joys,
Hanging all torn, she sees; and in His woes
And pains, her pangs and throes:
Each wound of His, from every part,
All, more at home in her one heart.

(ll. 1–10)

II

. . . While with a faithful, mutual flood,
Her eyes bleed tears, His wounds weep blood.

(ll. 19–20)

III

. . . His nails write swords in her, which soon
       her heart
     Pays back, with more than their own
       smart;
Her swords, still growing with His pain,
Turn spears, and straight come home again.

(ll. 27–30)

IV

She sees her Son, her God,
Bow with a load
Of borrowed sins; . . .

(ll. 31–33)

V

Oh mother turtle-dove!
Soft source of love! [4]

(ll. 41–42)

"This was the sky," points Thomas, as he turns to address familiarly the central actor of the drama. "This was the sky, Jack Christ, against which your cross loomed. This was the sky from which ministering angels should have descended to aid you, but they did not." The "minstrel angle" [5] is an ironic pun on the prophecy which Christ himself made when he said:

    . . . and they shall see the Son of man coming in the clouds of heaven with power and great glory.

97

And he shall send his angels with a great sound
of a trumpet and they shall gather together his
elect from the four winds, from one end of heaven
to the other.

(Matthew 24:30–31)

This was the divinely ordained event ("the heaven-
driven of the nails") which the Roman soldiers with
the instruments of the Passion—the hammer, nails, spear
—helped fulfill. The Cross looms against the sky so that
it appears as if the heavens, too, were nailed into the
crossbeams. The heaven-sent immensity once cloistered
in the womb is fastened to the finite dimensions of the
Cross, whose angles can be measured geometrically.
Each minstrel angle is the heaven-sent angle-iron or
nail, or the armored counterpart of the ministering
angels, the Roman soldiers, detailed by Pilate and God
to beat out the rhythmic sounds of hammerhead on
nail. We do not see the Son of Man coming in great
glory with arms outspread; instead, we see him with
arms stretched in sharp right angles on the Cross. Una-
muno, in *The Christ of Velázquez*, says of the Cross:
". . . it is the angle iron of our uprightness . . ." [6]

The geometry of Calvary is not complete without the
"three-coloured rainbow" arc issuing from Christ's nip-
ples, enveloping the sphere of earth from pole to pole.
The "snail-waked" world is slow to realize the meaning
of the Christian axiom: the sum total of the four right
angles of the Cross is 360 degrees. The whole globe is
contained in this sacrifice. [7]

The image of the rainbow arc of Christ's blood is
a reminder that the covenant made with Noah on Mount
Ararat is kept on Calvary. This second inundation saves
man; it does not destroy him. The image of the world
inundated by the flow of Christ's blood is the theme
of Crashaw's "Upon the Bleeding Crucifix: a Song":

This Thy blood's deluge (a dire chance,
    Dear Lord, to Thee) to us is found
A deluge of deliverance;

A deluge lest we should be drown'd.
Ne'er wast Thou in a sense so sadly true,
The well of living waters, Lord, till now.[8]
Thomas's rainbow is three-colored for several reasons.
He is consistent in sustaining his triads: the three cruci-
fied ones, the three Maries, the three trees, the three-
colored rainbow. Perhaps he was thinking of the three
primary colors: red, blue, and yellow. Actually, the
seven colors of the rainbow are rarely seen distinctly.
There is a considerable blurring, so that of the seven
colors three emerge: a red-orange, a yellow-green, and
a blue-violet. Dante describes the rainbow as three-
colored in *Paradiso* (Canto XXXIII, ll. 115–119):

In the deep, clear substance of that lofty light
three circles of three colors equal in diameter ap-
peared to me; and each reflected the other as rain-
bow mirroring rainbow . . .

In Book XI of *Paradise Lost* Milton mentions a three-
colored rainbow twice. Adam, in a vision of Noah safely
landed, rejoices over the rainbow in the sky:

A dewy cloud, and in the cloud a bow
Conspicuous with three listed colours gay
(ll. 865–866)

and Michael, concluding his remarks about the Flood,
speaks of God's "triple-coloured bow" (l. 897).

The account of the Crucifixion in the sonnet is con-
tinued after the nail and spear thrusts. Christ speaks
now as the divine surgeon, "all glory's sawbones," who
unsexes Death the skeleton, despoiling him of his sting.[9]
Here, between two thieves on the skull-shaped moun-
tain, at this moment, Christ is the death of Death. Una-
muno, too, in *The Christ of Velázquez* cries out: ". . .
and Thou wast the death of Death at the last!" Earlier
in the poem Unamuno speaks of Christ's generative
power: "In dying Thou didst beget, . . ." [10]

In Luke 4:23 Christ quotes a proverb ironically:
"Physician, heal thyself!" In this mountain minute "all
glory's sawbones," the divine physician, offers his own

99

body as oblation for the health of mankind. "The Physician slain . . . that the patient might recover!" exclaims Lancelot Andrewes in one of his Nativity sermons.[11] When Thomas alters "Suffer the little ones to come unto me" to "Suffer the heaven's children through my heartbeat," he combines Scripture and physiology to describe the act of redemption: Christ's dying heartbeat quickens all pulses.

The sense of "blowclock witness of the sun" is the extinction of time during the three hours of agony when nature herself, witness to the Crucifixion, darkens the world by eclipsing the sun. Donne, in his "Good friday, 1613. Riding Westward," makes use of an extended meteorological conceit of the eclipse and earthquake at the sixth hour:

What a death were it then to see God dye?
It made his owne Lieutenant Nature shrinke,
It made his footstoole crack, and the Sunne
    winke.

The conceit is further extended by the vocabulary of spheres, poles, hands, and zenith to measure time and space by the Crucifixion, the sun, and a clock. Thomas was as fascinated by modern mechanical devices, as a source of poetic imagery, as Donne was by the new cosmology. It is therefore possible that "blowclock" is a mechanical conceit, a neologism for timebomb. Thomas may have invented, for this occasion, a device which does not measure time but explodes it. At this "mountain minute" time is obliterated by an eclipse, and space is exploded by an earthquake in "blowclock witness" to the agony on Calvary. The image takes us back to an episode in the Old Testament, when the sun stood still long enough to assure Joshua victory in Jericho. But at this moment of defeat in Jerusalem, the sun disappears in the darkness of an eclipse.

All the drama and agony of the Passion are concentrated in this single sonnet. The prophecies in all the preceding sonnets have now been fulfilled. The gentleman of wounds, the long world's gentleman, is now the long world's wound. Here are the nettles and the horizontal crossbones of Abaddon. Now the lamb ascends the climbing grave on knocking knees, and here the crooked lad is twisted in the boneyards. Crossstroked and pin-legged, the second Adam is fastened to the rood, and through the wound of manwax the blood flows unstanched by gauze. No Lord's Prayer can help here, for the agonized cry is nothing but a scarecrow word. This is the Crucifixion on the mountain. This is the spearpoint of time which, like a gigantic indicator, registers doom. Genesis, birth, growth, love led to this mountain. For this moment in time a world was made, a tree planted, a Son begotten. And in this moment in time the Son is transfixed to the tree for the world.

9

Sonnet IX

Out of Egypt have I called my son.
Hosea 11:1 and Matthew 2:15

I shall not decay, I shall not rot, I shall not putrefy . . .
Chapter CLIV from
The Book of the Dead

THE NINTH SONNET seems to be composed of fourteen
lines of hieroglyphic verse to which even the Rosetta
stone is no key. One would expect the Crucifixion to be
followed by a sonnet centered on the descent from the
Cross; yet not a single traditional episode in the Passion
is offered. The first eight sonnets and the tenth form a
structural unity of Biblical narrative, Scriptural ref-
erences, and the motifs of Genesis, the Incarnation, and
the Passion. The ninth sonnet, however, is strikingly in-
congruent and seemingly disruptive of unity. It is as if
the long-vanished passion play of the life, death, and
resurrection of Osiris were to appear on Corpus Christi
Day between a pageant of the Crucifixion and a pageant
of the Last Judgment.

Why should a Welshman writing an English poem
about a Christian theme include a sonnet in which
there are detailed references to ancient Egyptian fu-
nerary customs and eschatology? This is not the only
instance of Thomas's use of imagery taken from Egyp-

tology. His published poems and unpublished manuscripts reveal a frequent preoccupation with Egyptian mythology and embalmment. One of his early attempts, at the age of sixteen, was a very lengthy poem called "Osiris Come to Isis" (MS, April, 1930). A brief quotation from this poem will illustrate a vocabulary and atmosphere repeated later in his first volume of poems:

> No parhelion in the Egypt skies,
> But symbol of the sun's fierce throat
> Steering its patriotic note
> Out of the air's blue boat . . .[1]

Thomas returned to the poem to salvage from it an astronomical term ("parhelion") for a stanza in a later poem:

> My world is pyramid. The padded mummer
> Weeps on the desert ochre and the salt
> Incising summer.
> My Egypt's armour buckling in its sheet,
> I scrape through resin to a starry bone
> And a blood parhelion.[2]

In two poems of his second volume, *Twenty-five Poems* (1936), Thomas used a vocabulary strikingly suggestive of more than a superficial knowledge of Egyptian embalmment and burial:

> Man was the scales, the death birds on
>   enamel,
> Tail, Nile, and snout, a saddler of the rushes,
> Time in the hourless houses
> Shaking the sea-hatched skull,
> And, as for oils and ointments on the flying
>   grail,
> All-hollowed wept for his white apparel.[3]

> Should lanterns shine, the holy face,
> Caught in an octagon of unaccustomed light,
> Would wither up, and any boy of love
> Look twice before he fell from grace.
> The features in their private dark

Are formed of flesh, but let the false day come
And from her lips the faded pigments fall,
And mummy cloths expose an ancient
   breast. . . .

So fast I move defying time; the quiet gentle-
   man
Whose beard wags in Egyptian wind.[4]
In his third volume of poems, *The Map of Love*
(1939), there is an even more ambitious use of Egyp-
tian mythology and embalmment terms:
Weighed in rock shroud, is my proud pyra-
   mid;
Where, wound in emerald linen and sharp
   wind,
The hero's head lies scraped of every legend,
Comes love's anatomist with sun-gloved hand
Who picks the live heart on a diamond.

"His mother's womb had a tongue that lapped
   up mud,"
Cried the topless, inchtaped lips from hank
   and hoof
In that bright anchorground where I lay lin-
   ened . . .[5]
The vocabulary of Egyptian archaeology undergoes a
metamorphosis into metaphor and pun, but the dis-
guised references give recognizable evidence of Thom-
as's sustained interest in Egyptian funerary customs.
The following brief list illustrates the transformation of
specific terms into poetic images:

"the padded mummer"	Padding used in mummies.
"Egypt's armour buckling in its sheet"	Outer covering of mummy or the mummy case.
"resin"	The gummy substance used in fixing strips of bandage into position; also used for stuffing bodies.

"death birds on enamel"	Probably the amulet of a vulture (*nerau-t*) which brought to the dead the protection of Isis; also an amulet of a man-headed hawk (*Ba*) typifying the soul of the dead.
"hourless houses"	Burial chambers.
"All-hollowed"	Pun on eviscerated corpse prepared for mummification.
"the live heart on a diamond"	The heart was removed and preserved in a jar. In its place was inserted a heart made of hard stone (carnelian, red jasper) or red faïence.

Why Thomas fashioned his imagery out of Egyptian mythology and necrology it is not difficult to understand. The recurrent theme of death and resurrection, the frequent anatomical imagery, the sustained sexual motif, and the ritual incantations in Thomas's poetry point to an explanation of his interest in Egyptian eschatology. All his familiar and frequent themes of birth, death, and rebirth are found in the Egyptian myths, the funerary customs, and the *Pyramid Texts*. The emphasis on sexuality is evident in the procreative motif in the Isis–Osiris legend, particularly in the ithyphallic representations of Osiris and Horus. The incantatory texts in the *Book of the Dead*, the ancient Egyptian funerary liturgy, and the passionate belief in immortality which marked Egyptian inscriptions, drama, and sculpture would appeal to a poet whose own lyrical deprecations against extinction echoed the horror of nothingness.

The preference, then, for Egyptian imagery may be accounted for, but the presence of this sonnet in the sequence is at first somewhat mystifying. How many of these lines were salvaged from Thomas's manuscripts it is hard to know. Several obvious facts in the sonnet, however, suggest its integral relationship to the poem. The burial motif is in chronological sequence to the Crucifixion in the preceding sonnet. There is an equal measure between "This was the crucifixion on the mountain" and "This was the resurrection in the desert." The furies to whom the "long gentleman" is wed are kin to the furies in attendance upon "the gentleman who lay graveward." And, finally, there is the contrast between the climactic, dynamic ascent in the eighth sonnet and the diminished intensity and movement of descent in the ninth.

This sonnet is much like the Egyptian ankh ☥ , or *crux ansata*, a symbol of immortality which later became the Coptic symbol of Christ's cross. This dual meaning of the ankh characterizes the sonnet. Perhaps Thomas, as he composed this part of the poem, recalled the verse "Out of Egypt have I called my son" (Hosea 11:1; Matthew 2:15), and in thinking of Egypt he saw the Passion of Christ implicit in the passion of Osiris. The parallel between the stories of the crucified Christ and the mutilated Osiris is apparent in the episodes of their life, death, and resurrection:

Osiris	*Christ*
1. Miraculous birth: son of the earth god Geb and sky goddess Nut; born on a day added to the Egyptian year of Thoth to avoid the curse of Ra.	1. Miraculous birth: son of God and Mary; saved from Herod's decree of the slaughter of the innocents.
2. Works of Osiris: cultivation of grains and the vine, introduction of the law.	2. Miracles wrought by Christ: water into wine, the miracle of the loaves and fishes, healing, "a new commandment I give unto you."

Osiris	*Christ*
3. The betrayal of Osiris by Set in the coffin ruse.	3. The betrayal of Christ by Judas.
4. The dismemberment of Osiris by Set into fourteen (some versions record fifteen, sixteen, or twenty-two) pieces.	4. The crucifixion and piercing of Christ.
5. The collection of the hacked parts of the body of Osiris, the embalmment, the mummification, the burial.	5. The descent from the Cross, Christ wrapped in linens, the embalmment in oils and spices, the burial in the tomb or cave (Matthew 27: 59–60; Mark 15:46; John 19:39–40).
6. The wailing and lamentation for Osiris by Isis and Nephthys.	6. The weeping of the three Maries.
7. The search for the body of Osiris.	7. The visit of the three Maries to the tomb.
8. The resurrection of Osiris in the spring, in the desert. The Shemut season (rise of the Nile) takes place, according to Egyptologists, on March 16. The rise of the Nile is a symbol of immortality to all who die. The Egyptian dead were given the name of Osiris as prefix, since they partook of his attribute of life everlasting.	8. The resurrection of Christ in spring in the Palestinian desert. The significance of rebirth through baptism in the Jordan. The promise of salvation and eternal life to all who die in Christ.

The imagery and function of the sonnet are not nearly as puzzling as the technical vocabulary. Where did

Thomas learn of Egyptian embalmment, mummification, eschatology? I believe the ninth sonnet may owe its origin to a work called *The Mummy*, a study of Egyptian embalmment and burial customs, written by E. A. Wallis Budge, late keeper of the Department of Egyptian and Assyrian Antiquities in the British Museum.[6] I have quoted a series of excerpts from Budge together with those phrases and lines from the ninth sonnet which indicate a striking similarity to the material in Budge's work. (The page numbers refer to *The Mummy* except in one instance where a quotation is taken from Budge's *From Fetish to God*.)

> *From the oracular archives and the parch-*
>   *ment,*
> *Prophets and fibre kings in oil and letter,*
> *The lamped calligrapher . . .*

On the back of the parchment sheath [found in a tomb in Upper Egypt] is a design, stamped in black ink, . . . (p. 176)
The ink . . . was . . . contained in a pad of vegetable fibre or linen, . . . (p. 176)
The black ink . . . is commonly supposed to have been made of lamp black, . . . (p. 176)
In the case of a king the oils were presented in alabaster flasks [in the anointing of the dead] . . . (p. 238)
Oil or unguent for anointing the body was almost as necessary for the Egyptians as food, . . . (p. 265)

> *. . . the queen in splints,*
> *Buckle to lint and cloth their natron footsteps,*

The body was entirely covered with linen and laid upon a board, . . . (p. 217)
The . . . mummy-board is a flat wooden covering

. . . of the same shape and size as the mummy on which it was laid . . . (p. 219)

. . . they steep the body in natron for the prescribed number of days, . . . the natron dissolves the flesh, and nothing . . . remains but the skin and bones. (pp. 204–205)

When a body has been preserved by natron, . . . the skin is found to be hard . . . (p. 208)

. . . thick pads of linen are laid on the top of the feet . . . [This was to prevent injury to the feet when the mummy was placed in an upright position.] (p. 344)

Draw on the glove of prints, . . .

. . . it was customary to inscribe texts upon the mummy cloths, and . . . large vignettes accompany the Chapters from the Book of the Dead; . . . (p. 216)

The outer sheets were wound around the mummy, not drawn on like a sack or glove as Thomas suggests.

Draw on the glove of prints, dead Cairo's
     henna
Pour like a halo on the caps and serpents.

It is equally certain that . . . [the Egyptian lady] stained the nails of her fingers and toes with *hinnâ* . . . [which was contained in a jar placed in the tomb of the mummy for use in the other world]. (p. 266)

The nails of the hands are tinted with *hinnâ* . . . (p. 343)

The head [of the deceased] was provided with a band or cap, . . . (p. 217)

The king [Seti I of the XIXth dynasty] is shown wearing . . . royal head-dress, with a uraeus over the forehead, . . . [The uraeus, or serpent, was a part of the diadem worn by royalty as a symbol of sovreignty.] (p. 254)

This was the resurrection in the desert, . . .
With priest and pharaoh bed my gentle
*   wound,*

The resurrection of the dead was assured by planting the "grain-bed of Osiris" in the tomb. The bed was made of layers of papyrus upon which moistened earth was spread, sown with barley grains in a figure of Osiris. Aided by the moisture in the darkness of the tomb, the barley grains sprouted, thus outlining a "living" form of Osiris. This symbolic resurrection of the god implied the resurrection of the occupant of the tomb, since the barley represented not only Osiris but the deceased as well. Thus entrance into the kingdom of the gods and of the blessed spirits was assured the soul of the dead. Budge describes the barley grain as "the dead Osiris" and the barley sproutings as "Osiris who, in the form of living plants, had risen from the dead." (p. 462)

Death from a bandage, . . .

And now the bandaging begins. The body is first of all smeared over with unguents. Pieces of linen are torn into strips . . . and one edge of each strip is gummed . . . The embalmers having bandaged the fingers, hands, and arms, and toes separately, begin to bandage the body from the feet upwards . . . On these fine linen bandages passages from the Book of the Dead, and formulae which were intended to give power to the dead, are written . . . (pp. 343–344)
. . . a coarse piece of linen is laid on the body and is sewn up at the back. Over this . . . a saffron-coloured linen sheet is laid, and . . . deftly sewn over the head, down the back, and under the feet, . . . held in position by a perpendicular bandage of . . . linen, . . . (p. 345)

Gold on such features, . . .

Over the face [of the mummy] is inserted a portrait of the deceased, with a golden laurel crown on his head; on the breast, in gold, is a collar, . . . The scenes painted in gold on the body are: . . . Anubis, Isis, and Nephthys at the bier of the deceased; . . . The bodies of children . . . have traces of gilding upon them . . . And mummies of children have the hair curled and gilded, . . . (pp. 212–213)
. . . many Egyptians . . . [provided] the dead with . . . head cases having gilded faces . . . (p. 221)
The face [of the mummy] is gilded. (p. 222)
. . . and a curious feature of the cover [of the anthropoid coffin of a king's scribe] is that the beard is gilded. (p. 258)

Weds my long gentleman to dusts and furies;

The body of Osiris having been brought into a special place in the temple, was next taken to the chamber in which his resurrection was to take place. But it was thought that devils and evil spirits might attack the body, and in addition to the priests who were in the chamber always ready to protect the body, a guard of gods was established to ward off evil influences and the attacks of devils. [A description of the "secret mysteries" or dramatic re-enactment of the resurrection of Osiris in Budge's *From Fetish to God*, p. 504.] [7]

World in the sand, . . .

Sometimes the body was wrapped loosely in a coarse linen cloth and buried in a hole dug in the sand, . . . (p. 336)

With stones of odyssey for ash and garland
And rivers of the dead around my neck.

> . . . necklaces . . . [of semi-precious stones] were
> worn by the living and the dead . . . necklaces
> were supposed to bring protection and well-being
> to their wearers. Every stone was believed to pos-
> sess . . . magical power or influence . . . (p. 266)

Among a long list of amulets Budge includes the amulet
of the serpent's head, a uraeus, which he describes as
follows:

> This amulet is made of red jasper, . . . and other
> reddish stones. It represented Isis as the great
> serpent-goddess, and was placed inside the wrap-
> pings of mummies and attached to their necks to
> prevent their being devoured by worms in the
> tombs. (pp. 322–323)

The ancient Egyptians believed that the dead had to
cross a river in their odyssey to the Island of Osiris:

> But the route by land [where the departed dwelt]
> was . . . interrupted by a river, which the dead
> had to cross, and the heaven that they hoped to
> reach was intersected by canals and streams. There-
> fore it was . . . necessary to provide the dead
> with boats in the Other World. This was done by
> making models of boats and putting them in the
> tombs with the dead, so that when they arrived at
> the great river in the Tuat [Other World] . . . the
> spirit of the boat might convey the soul to the place
> where it fain would be. (pp. 463–464)

The sestet begins with a procession of prophets,
anointed kings, a scribe, and a queen. From the ancient
pyramid texts and papyrus documents emerges a record
of a civilization long dead. The "oracular archives"
which had once foretold the immortality of the mummi-
fied royal persons become now relics of the past rather
than oracles of the future. No longer are the bodies
held together by living sinews and muscles bound to

112

bone; instead, flesh has been dissolved in natron, and skin and bones have been bound by linen fibers of mummy cloths on which are inscribed, in hieratic and hieroglyphic characters, the prayers for the well-being of the dead in the other world. The prophets' visions and the kings' splendor are wrapped in linen and solidified in sodium carbonate. The court scribe, whose calligraphy in lamp black ("lamped calligrapher") appeared on papyrus rolls and mummy cloths, and whose illumination of vignettes brightened the *Book of the Dead*, now lies in bandaged stillness next to his palette, writing reed, and inkpots. And the queen no longer sits upon her throne but lies, eviscerated and linen-wrapped, between the mummy boards ("the queen in splints").

All the dead—the royal, the priestly, the scribal—are discovered by Thomas in the process of preserving themselves, as if they had become animated in the archives and pyramid texts. Their static procession in the stylized stance of Egyptian statuary, one foot directly in front of the other, is described by "natron footsteps." The mood of the verbs "buckle," "draw on," "pour" is indicative, giving the reader the sense that he is observing these ancient figures embalming and adorning themselves for their journey into eternity. Each verb is chosen deliberately to suggest both a contemporary action of a living person and a funerary custom observed by ancient Egyptians. "Buckle to lint and cloth their natron footsteps" brings to our eye the image of someone buckling on his overshoes, and at the same time we see mummies buckling or binding their petrified feet with linen bandages to the rest of their bodies. "Draw on the glove of prints" suggests someone putting on a glove or drawing chintz covers over furniture until we realize that the reference is to the vignette-decorated outer coverings of linen which conformed glovelike to the shape of the mummy. And lastly, ". . . dead Cairo's henna / Pour like a halo . . ." offers a cosmetic image of a hair rinse; but "dead Cairo" reminds us of the ancient technique of tinting the hair of a mummy with henna and of adorning the head with a band or diadem in the form of a uraeus. We know, for example, that the hair of the mummy of Queen Henttawi (XVIIIth dynasty) was dyed a brilliant reddish color, probably of henna stain.[8] "Dead Cairo" expresses the necrological civilization which Thomas describes in the imagery of embalming and burial, or it might be a geographical synecdoche for Egypt.

The tone of the first six lines of the sonnet recalls Ecclesiastes and Shelley's "Ozymandias"; time and dust and corruption mock kings, prophets, and scribes. Crowns, oracles, art, beauty are all treasures which moths, rust, wind, and sand corrupt and corrode. And the flesh, like its adornments, despite natron and linen bandages, remains corruptible. Recalling the defeat in the line "This was the crucifixion on the mountain," Thomas introduces the octave of the ninth sonnet with "This was the resurrection in the desert," commenting ironically on the archaeological resurrection of the dead by the scholars, who are revealed to us in an Epiphany of modern Wise Men, uttering exclamations over a discovery in an opened tomb. Syntax and punctuation offer difficulties which are easily resolved if a comma is assumed to have been omitted after "scholars." Thomas has arranged two scenes through montage: the collective scholars are represented by a single mask behind which they "rant" in their amazement over the accomplishments of the ancient Egyptians in keeping "Death from a bandage." The scholars' wonder at the attempt of the corruptible to put on incorruption is extended to their admiration of the "gold on such features": the gilded faces, hair, and beards of the mummies, their gold accouterments, their amulets, pectorals, rings, and bracelets. The word "rant" is an explicit indication of Thomas's attitude toward the scholars who disturb the long sleep and wake the mummies to a resurrection in a museum or monograph. The mask is another example of Thomas's ability to produce multiple effects with one image. The mask may suggest a staged drama of discovery in the desert.[9] It may simply be the masks which archaeological excavators wear as dust filters. It may also suggest a surgical image, an effect produced by the dust masks of the archaeologists, who stand over the discovered mummy like so many surgeons over an anesthetized patient. And lastly, there is the grotesque contrast between the living wearing dust masks and the dead wearing painted masks.

In this desert Passion play "the linen spirit" is a less substantial member of the cast than either the mummies or the scholars. The definite article establishes the spirit as a kind of resident genius of the tombs and graves. It may be a *ka* or double given form and substance by being wound in linen bandages.[10] The spirit is a macabre matchmaker, the Egyptian counterpart of Abaddon in the earlier sonnets. The nuptials of the tomb are performed by the spirit between the long gentleman (Christ) and the dust and furies. The "furies," as Thomas calls them, are desert demons against whom

. . . both the mummified body and the spiritual elements which had inhabited it upon earth ["linen spirit"] had to be protected from a multitude of devils and fiends, and from the powers of darkness generally. These powers of evil had hideous and terrifying shapes and forms, and their haunts were well known, for they infested the region through which the road of the dead lay when passing from this world to the Kingdom of Osiris.[11]

The last four lines of the sonnet are burial instructions. The possessive pronoun belongs to Thomas, who has taken possession of Christ and his wound. But in these sonnets possession is shared, and the pronoun belongs to Christ, too, who asks that his wound (body) be bedded gently in the sand, where he will mingle with priest and Pharaoh who have long before preceded him. There is a sad incantatory tone in the burial directions, and even a weary pun in the echo of "world without end" in "world in the sand."

There are two kingdoms of death: the world in the sand, the "triangle landscapes" or pyramid tombs in the desert, which contain the mummy; and there is death's other kingdom, the land of resurrection beyond rivers which the dead must cross. The long odyssey beyond the rivers is beset with many hazards; therefore the dead god asks that amulets be hung around his neck ("With stones of odyssey for . . . garland") to make certain of his arrival in the Tuat, or other world. These amulets are offered by mourners for the protection of the dead and are also given in gratitude for the eternal life promised the spirit. There are carvings on these amulets which depict scenes of the spirits' journey; there are also inscriptions of prayers for the well-being of the deceased.

The "rivers of the dead" have a place in the *Pyramid Texts* as they do in the literature of the Coptic Christians. Budge describes the Egyptian and Christian counterparts of Charon. According to Egyptian eschatology the souls were ferried across the rivers by the ferryman of Osiris, Herefhaf, who would only ferry the souls of the righteous to the Island of Osiris. Coptic Christian belief in the afterworld reflected the myth of rivers and ferryman found in the Book of the Dead. Thus we have an account in the Coptic Apocrypha about a gift of a boat, given to John the Baptist by Christ, to ferry souls across the river in Amente [12] (the Coptic afterworld borrowed from the Egyptians):

> And I have given the boat of gold to John My Kinsman, for the passage over the river, so that he may be able to transport therein those who shall celebrate his commemoration upon the earth, if it be only by breaking a little bread, and the pouring out of a [little] cold water. [13]

The "stones of odyssey," the talismans or amulets for the journey of the dead, will serve in place of "ash and garland." Thomas combines several burial customs in this single line: the ash is from the Anglican burial service: "earth to earth, ashes to ashes, dust to dust." The garland is a reminder of other slain and resurrected gods: the wreaths of violets woven for the tree trunk, swathed like a corpse, in commemoration of the death of Attis; the grain sprouting from the effigies of Osiris; and the miniature pot gardens planted in memory of Adonis. The ash and garland become the soundless lament over the dead god and the rejoicing over his resurrection. All the slain and resurrected gods are merged here in the archetypal Osiris. The tomb of Osiris becomes all tombs: the pyramid, sandpit, cave. The lament of Isis for Osiris becomes the lament of Aphrodite for Adonis, of Astarte for Tammuz, of Cybele for Attis, and finally of the dolorous mother for the pierced Son. All wounds become one wound: the dismemberment of Osiris, the boar's wounding of Adonis, the mutilation of Attis, and the Crucifixion of Christ. And all resurrections become one resurrection in the spring, assuring men of the power of life over darkness and dust; giving promise of the quickening of that which, unless it die, cannot live. The ninth sonnet is a poem in miniature of Sir James Frazer's analysis of the Attis, Osiris, Tammuz, and Adonis legend. To Sir James these gods are ". . . a god of many names but of essentially one nature . . ." [14] A passage in *The Golden Bough* sums up for us the theme of this sonnet:

> Under the names of Osiris, Tammuz, Adonis, and Attis, the peoples of Egypt and Western Asia represented the yearly decay and revival of life, especially of vegetable life, which they personified as a god who annually died and rose again from the dead. In name and detail the rites varied from place to place: in substance they were the same. [15]

The "rivers of the dead" are not only the rivers along which the souls travel to reach the other kingdom; they are also a confluence of the life-giving waters of the

Adonis River, the Nile, the Jordan. And lest we have forgotten that this is a "Christian voyage," we are reminded that all rivers flow home to the sea. It is in the tenth sonnet that we resume the "Christian voyage" on the imaged seas.

10

Sonnet X

For though through many straits, and lands I roame,
I launch at paradise, and I sail toward home;
        John Donne, "The Progress of the Soul"

Then the most beloved Son of God, Christ, descending on
earth shall lead thy father Adam to Paradise to the tree of
mercy.
        The Books of Adam and Eve
        (in the Pseudepigrapha) 42:5

WHETHER THOMAS meant the tenth sonnet to be a temporary pause or a full stop, we cannot know. He himself, as we have seen, described the religious sonnets as the "first passage of. . . a very long poem"; and a note in *Twenty-five Poems* described the sonnets as a poem which "contains the first ten sections of a work in progress." [1] The tenth sonnet takes us beyond the narrative content of the first nine sonnets in the same way that the books of the Acts of the Apostles and Revelation take us beyond the narrative theme of the synoptic Gospels.

There is a suspension of the laws of nature and of syntax in the tenth sonnet. Ubiquitous pronouns lurk mysteriously with no antecedents to give them ancestry; yet subjects seem to belong to verbs, and possessive pronouns are attracted to nouns. Bodies of water are unreal; yet they are defined hydrographically as bay, chan-

119

nel, and harbor. Meteorological aberrations occur, too: there are winged harbors and a garden diving and flying. St. Peter, in a strategic position suggesting the suspension of evangelic disbelief, surveys strange prodigies: a fish potentially capable of answering a riddle; a submerged anthropomorphic rhubarb; a serpent behaving like a bird; [2] and a sunken garden soaring heavenward.

The population in the sonnet, except for St. Peter, is audible but invisible. Who then are the tale's sailor, the globe balancer, the sea imager, the tall fish, the rhubarb man? Who commands in the first ten lines? Who prays in the last four lines? Is the geography a Mercator's projection, or is it the geography of Revelation? And what of time: is it meridian, historical, millennial? Perhaps the answers may be found in the imagery and structure of the sonnet.

Structurally the sonnet is divided into three parts: a voyage, a riddle, and a prayer; each part is introduced by the word "let." The first part is advisory and purposive: the tale's sailor is advised to anchor off the bay in order to accomplish a certain purpose. The second part is hortatory and inquisitive: Peter is urged to ask the tall fish a question. The third part is precatory and conclusive: a prayer is chanted for the advent of Judgment Day, which will bring to fulfillment a prophecy of the heavenly kingdom and life everlasting in the green garden. The last two parts are related to each other by the image of the garden; the first part, however, seems to stand alone. If we place the sequence of events in the New Testament parallel to the events in this sonnet, and if we understand the words "bible east" to mean the direction from which Christianity spread (east to west), the sonnet becomes unified in theme and imagery.

The Voyage

Is the "Christian voyage" an account of a religious journey, or is it a metaphor of the poem itself? It may be both. It is possible, since Thomas had planned a very long poem, that he chose the tenth sonnet as a temporary anchorage. I prefer to think that the "Christian voyage" is a series of meditations based on Biblical episodes, with the tenth sonnet marking the journey's end in a vision and prayer.

The first ten lines of the sonnet reveal Christ calling Peter to witness the triumph of faith over doubt in the example of Paul. The nautical imperative to the "tale's sailor" comes from Christ himself, who as harbormaster presides over the action in the sonnet. The nautical feat to be accomplished: "hold halfway off the dummy bay" reminds one of Luke's wonder: "What manner of man is this? for he commandeth even the winds and water, and they obey him" (Luke 8:25). The tale's sailor is a seagoing evangel who has undertaken a voyage in imitation of Christ. I think he is that indefatigable sailor, St. Paul, putting into various ports after calms, storms, and shipwrecks; preaching to those who have come to "spot the blown word." An examination of Acts 27:9–37, in which Paul proves his seamanship, might explain how, almost literally, Paul tried to "hold halfway off the dummy bay" the ship on which he had set sail for Rome. His admonition to the centurion and officers of the ship, the account of the storm, the attempt to land the boat in the bay, the running aground on a sandbar ("dummy bay"), and the pounding to pieces of the boat ("ship-racked gospel") seem to be the theme of the first three lines. The balanced globe is Christ's burden, the same burden his disciples are asked to bear "atlaswise."

"Time's ship-racked gospel" is pun and prophecy; it is also a reversal of the earlier episodes in the sequence. We are witness to the translation of time into eternity as earlier in the sonnets we were witness to eternity translated into time. The "ship-racked gospel" or "blown word" is a metaphor of the paradigm of salvation: the New Testament. Metaphor is extended by a versatile pun: "ship-racked" is literally Paul's storm-tossed ship ("racked" is a nautical term describing the swaying of a ship from side to side); it is Paul's shipwreck and Paul's racked body—he is scourged and beaten and finally executed. The "blown word" may be the divine *pneuma*, the Gospel propelled by wind in the sails, and also Paul's eloquence.

The colon at the end of the third line brings the navigation image to a close. The word "so" in the next line suggests that what follows will be the result of heeding the nautical admonition. Curious folk, attracted by the rockbirds hovering over the vessel offshore, will come to see ("spot") the "ship-racked gospel" and hear the "blown word." The "winged harbours" at first suggest Swift's flying island of Laputa, but only if we see them as meteorological aberrations. "Winged harbours" is a trope describing the harbors filled with flying birds, the rockbirds. Milton, in *Comus* (1. 730), speaks of "the wing'd air dark't with plumes" to suggest bird-crowded skies. The harbors are the ports of call to which the harbingers of the Word come.

"Rockbirds" is another instance of Thomas's ingenuity. As harbor fauna the rockbirds sustain the shore imagery. As metaphor they suggest the curious populace on the rocky beaches and jetties come to hear the Gospel. And as a play on words the rockbirds imply the tempestuous careers of Peter and Paul, the stormy petrels, in the Gospels. One of the definitions of rockbird is "cock of the rock." When one remembers that the cock and the rock are associated with Peter, and when we discover Peter in the octave of the sonnet, we can understand Thomas's choice of "rockbirds." The fisher of fish was first known by his Hebrew name of Simon bar Jonah (Simon, son of the dove); when he became a fisher of men, he was called Cephas or Peter (from *petros*, rock, the Greek equivalent of the Aramaic *cephas*).[3]

The "seas I image" is a counterweight to "the globe I balance." It is also Christ's statement of the universality of his message, which, like the seas, touches all shores where winter solstice and Saturnalia have been transformed into the commemoration of Nativity and Passion ("December's thorn screwed in a brow of holly"), the two events in time requisite for redemption in eternity. In leaving the sestet we leave time: the octave is of eternity.

The Riddle

The octave begins with the second imperative exhorting Peter to ask the tall fish a riddle. He is the "first Peter" because his primacy in the Gospels was established by Jesus himself. He is also the first apostle encountered in Heaven. That he is in Heaven in the sonnet is made evident by the rainbow railing, an appropriate material for a protective guard in the infinite dimensions of heaven. Peter is not at the gates; he is on a heavenly quay. Thomas has made use of a setting and riddle which sustain the taunting tone evident in those episodes of the Gospels and Acts involving Peter and Christ, and Peter and Paul. We must remember that Peter's faith was often weakened by fear. Thomas has already suggested this in the phrase "wind-turned statement" (sonnet VII) referring to Peter's denial of Christ. Now we are reminded of the water and fish miracles.[4] With deft irony Thomas has assigned Peter to a place in Heaven where his previous occupation will make him feel at home, and where he will remember eternally the numerous lessons he had to learn repeatedly on earth. The quay is a safe place for a fisherman like Peter, and a railed quay is a necessary safeguard for one who is seized with panic in a boat during a storm. The rainbow is also an excellent reminder, to one of wavering faith, of God's sign of a promise made to a more substantial boatman than Peter—Noah.

The identity of the speaker who bids Peter ask the fish a riddle is ambiguous. The speaker may be the poet, Jesus, or Paul. The words of the puzzled evil spirit in

123

Acts 19:15 are most appropriate to the ambiguity of this section: "Jesus I know, and Paul I know; but who are ye?" I believe the speaker in the sonnet is Jesus, reminding Peter that the Christian voyage would not have become universal had it not been for Paul. It was Peter who wanted to restrict the Messianic ideal to the Jews alone; it was Paul who preached it to all men. In the Gospels the word is preached inland; in the Acts and Epistles the word reaches beyond the seas.

The "tall fish" should be no surprise to Peter. On one occasion he hooked a fish with a gold stater in its mouth for payment of taxes (Matthew 17:27). On another occasion he hauled in a net of one hundred and fifty-three big fish (John 21:11). The "tall fish," then, is a reminder that he was always provided for.[5] That is why the resurrected Christ, after Peter's substantial breakfast of fish, reminds him to "feed my sheep." The taunting tone of the riddle in the sonnet is an echo of Christ taunting Peter when he asked him, at that breakfast scene, "Lovest thou me?" three times. Peter is not obtuse, for we learn that he was grieved because he was asked the same question three times—once for each denial.

The fish "swept from the bible east" is also a metaphor of the expansion of Christianity from east to west, the result of Paul's missions. And finally, as a symbol derived from an acrostic, the fish represents Christ. The Greek word *ichthus* (fish) or ΙΧΘΥΣ forms an acrostic which reads Ἰησοῦς Χριστός Θεοῦ Υἱός Σωτήρ (Jesus Christ, Son of God, the Savior). Tertullian in one of his lighter moments puns when he speaks of Christians as ". . . little fishes after the image of our ΙΧΘΥΣ . . ."[6] The numerous examples in comparative folklore of Peter's encounter with the fish containing the stater are convincing testimony of the efficacy of Paul's transformation of a local cult into a universal religion. The fish (*Zeus faber*), which is a golden yellow color, is common in the Mediterranean. Greek fishermen call it *Christopsaro* or "Christfish"; Italians call it *sanpiero* or in more leisurely moments *pesce de San Pietro;* to Germans it is *der Petersfisch;* and to the French *le poisson de St. Pierre.* Among the Gascons the fish is called the golden or sacred cock—a marvelous instance of folk metaphor fusing two incidents in Peter's life! And since the fish is also native to the waters around the southwestern coasts of England, English fishermen recognize it as the "John dory" (possibly from French *dorée,* golden, and *jaune,* yellow). The fish was Peter's; the faith was Paul's.

If the Biblical and acrostical attributes of the fish identify it, its syntactical ambiguity makes it very elusive. The fish is described as "tall," an unusual adjective for a creature which exists in the horizontal. Thomas probably combined three meanings of the word in one. Fish stories are "tall" stories, and Peter was involved in at least two such tall tales. Tall also means fine, and it means long.[7] The size of the fish may be in keeping with Peter's fishing exploits, but why is the fish female? I take the phrase "in her foam-blue channel" to refer to the habitat of the tall fish. I think the fish is female because Thomas may have wanted to suggest the triumph of St. Paul over Venus: the *agape* of Paul proved stronger than the *eros* of Venus. The foam-blue channel recalls the birth of Venus from the foam of the sea, and the submerged garden reminds us that there was a cult of Venus in Rome, where she was worshiped as the goddess of beauty and gardens. Her cult was powerful and widespread; yet the peeled rhubarb man, with his promise of another garden and his words about a love which surpassed understanding, swept her out of the east. Is it not a significant coincidence that St. Paul's first missionary journey should have been to Cyprus, that island which gave the ancient poets the epithet Cyprian for Venus? And perhaps it is an even more significant coincidence that at Paphos (on Cyprus), where a cult of Venus flourished, Saul changed his name to Paul. And when he came as a prisoner to Rome, the city in which Venus was powerfully established, it was the rhubarb man who supplanted her. He had made of her, indeed, a "sea-ghost": the dolphin, sacred to Venus, became the symbol of Christ; her garden became the longed-for Eden; her star became *Stella Maris;* and even her name day, *Dies Veneris,* became the day on which the commemorative meal of fish is eaten.

The riddle, restated in prose, is simply this: Who is the rhubarb man peeled in the foam-blue waters of the eastern Mediterranean? In its tone and context the riddle suggests rebuke, taunt, and triumph. Apparently Peter can understand riddles as long as they are connected with fish. Thomas's vegetable image is chosen not because rhubarb has an exotic, Oriental history. He wanted a vegetable which, by the reddish color of its long stalks, might suggest the long wound (sonnet VIII) of the Crucifixion. And he wanted a vegetable which by its bitter leaves and high acid content would describe the acerb qualities of St. Paul. The vegetable as epithet is used by Sir Philip Sidney to suggest bitterness in his line "But with your rhubarb word ye must contend." [8] We associate Paul with *agape* and the exaltation of love in I Corinthians (13:1–13), forgetting that he was, indeed, a rhubarb man on numerous occasions. He could be withering in his contempt, irony, and abuse. A glance at his epistles (particularly II Corinthians, Galatians, and Philippians) will reveal his acidulous temper. It was of Peter and his church of Jerusalem that he was especially contemptuous.

The phrase "peeled in her foam-blue channel" possibly describes the numerous scourgings of Paul in his missions in the eastern Mediterranean (at least eight times, according to his own account in II Corinthians 11:24, 25). The riddle implies that it was Paul who had sown the belief in bodily resurrection and life everlasting in Paradise, thereby reaping innumerable conversions and assuring the success of the new religion. The word "peeled" suggests the very wordplay of Paul himself in his controversy with Peter over circumcision as a requisite for admission of the Gentiles to the confraternity of believers.[9] The eventual victory of Paul over Peter in this controversy resulted in the spread of the movement from the hills of Judaea to the hills of Rome and beyond.

The "sea-ghost" is the ironic reminder to Peter that it was he who, along with the other disciples, believing Christ was a ghost, called out for proof: "Lord, if it be thou, bid me come unto thee on the water" (Matthew 14:28). To Paul, however, Christ was not a sea-ghost: he was the hypostasis of Paul's faith, and it was that faith around which the garden flourished. Whether Thomas knew more about rhubarb than its color and flavor, I do not know. Of more than horticultural interest to the reader of the poem is the fact that rhubarb seeds do not produce plants true to the variety that bears them. In order to propagate the variety of the parent plant, it is necessary to cut its perennial crown into pieces, each piece consisting of a root and a bud. Since Paul was a Roman citizen, his martyrdom was not crucifixion but execution by the sword. Legend holds that he was beheaded. He was indeed a rhubarb man. A look at the rhubarb flower reveals an interesting symbolism: the flower is white, containing three-angled or winged fruits of one seed each. Sermons may be found in stones, and theology in botany.

The Prayer

There is no pause between the second and third parts of the sonnet. The vision of the flying garden introduces the incantatory prayer of the last four lines. The green leaves and red stalk of the rhubarb, the spiny leaves and bright berries of the holly, and the green beginning and red tree illustrate the paradox of the bloody agony and green immortality. The visions in Isaiah and Revelation are the source of the moving prayer offered by Christ or Thomas or both:

127

The wolf also shall dwell with the lamb, and
the leopard shall lie down with the kid . . .
And the sucking child shall play on the hole
of the asp, and the weaned child shall put his
hand on the adder's den. They shall not hurt
nor destroy in all my holy mountain . . .

(Isaiah 11:6–9

He will swallow up death in victory; and the
Lord God will wipe away tears from all
faces . . .

(Isaiah 25:8)

And he showed me a pure river of water of life,
clear as crystal proceeding out of the throne of
God and of the Lamb. In the midst of the
street of it, and on either side of the river, was
there the tree of life . . . and the leaves of
the tree were for the healing of the nations.

(Revelation 22:1, 2)

And God shall wipe away all tears from their
eyes; and there shall be no more death,
neither sorrow, nor pain: for the former things
are passed away.

(Revelation 21:4)

The tenth sonnet unifies the entire sequence by echo-
ing the word combinations of the first sonnet. "Altar-
wise" and "atlas-eater" become "atlaswise"; and "atlas-
eater" is recalled in "the globe I balance"; "half-way
house" and "half-way winds" become "hold half-way
off"; the "walking word" is now the "blown word." Cer-
tain images of the last sonnet are paired with those of
the first. The anthropomorphic, bitten-out mandrake is
joined by the peeled rhubarb man. The explicit Abad-
don, the Angel of Destruction, remains in the Bottom-
less Pit; Gabriel, the Angel of Resurrection, implicit
in the last four lines of the tenth sonnet, soars with the
flying garden. "That night of time" now becomes "that
Day," and "the windy salvage" is "the nest of mercies."

The Christward shelter in Bethlehem toward which the Word descended is now the Christward mansion toward which the prayer ascends. "Altarwise," the first word of the first sonnet, implies the sacrifice which brings redemption through the "tree," the last word of the last sonnet. The architecture of this poem can be seen in Thomas's use of the letters A and T. Originally the letter tau (T) was the final letter of the Greek alphabet, not omega (Ω). Herrick, in the concluding couplet to his *Noble Numbers* makes use of *alpha–tau,* as beginning and end:

Of all the good things whatso'ere we do
God is the ΑΡΧΗ [beginning], and the ΤΕΛΟΣ
[end] too.

Prosody is always at work in the sonnets; and so is prophecy.

The prayer with which the poem concludes rises with the hope that the flying garden, green as Eden, submerged for so long, will now rise to the surface of the sea. In the prayer there is a vision. The two trees ("the two bark towers"), Adam's tree and Christ's tree, will rise and become one tree around which the serpent once more will coil, bringing not venom but golden straws to build a "nest of mercies" for the Dove. And this nest will be woven in the rude, red tree of ignominious death upon which the Dove was once transfixed. Here, at last, the covenant will be redeemed, the promise fulfilled, innocence restored, death banished. The poem ends in a hymn of faith, a prayer of hope, and a vision of love.

Notes

The abbreviation *CP* stands for the American edition of Thomas's *Collected Poems*. The number in parentheses following *CP* is the page number.

INTRODUCTION.

[1] Dylan Thomas, "Wilfred Owen," *Quite Early One Morning* (New York: New Directions, 1954), p. 126.

[2] BBC program, *Freedom Forum*, "What Has Happened to English Poetry?" A discussion between Edward Shanks and Dylan Thomas with Anthony McDonald as chairman, Oct. 16, 1946.

[3] Edith Sitwell, "Four New Poets," *London-Mercury*, Vol. XXXIII (Feb., 1936), p. 386.

[4] Herbert J. C. Grierson and J. C. Smith, *A Critical History of English Poetry* (New York: Oxford University Press, 1946), p. 566.

[5] Robert Lowell, "Thomas, Bishop, and Williams," *Sewanee Review*, Vol. LV, no. 3 (Summer, 1947), pp. 493–496.

[6] Leslie Fiedler, "The Latest Dylan Thomas," *Western Review*, Vol. XI, no. 2 (Winter, 1947), pp. 103–106.

[7] Thomas, letter to the editors, *Life and Letters Today*, XIII (Dec., 1935), p. 232.

[8] Thomas, *Letters to Vernon Watkins*, ed. by Vernon Watkins (London: J. M. Dent and Faber and Faber, 1957), pp. 13–14.

[9] Henry Treece, "The Poet Answers a Critic," in *Dylan Thomas* (London: Lindsay Drummond, 1949), pp. 149–150. Quotation of comments by Dylan Thomas referring to a review of his poems by Edith Sitwell in the *Sunday Times* of November 15, 1936 (p. 9).

[10] Francis Scarfe, "Dylan Thomas: A Pioneer," in *Auden and After: The Liberation of Poetry 1930–1941* (London: George Routledge, 1942), p. 106.

[11] David Daiches, "The Poetry of Dylan Thomas," in *Literary Essays* (Edinburgh and London: Oliver and Boyd, 1956), p. 57.

[12] Elder Olson, *The Poetry of Dylan Thomas* (Chicago: University of Chicago Press, 1954), p. 64.

[13] Tindall, William York, *A Reader's Guide to Dylan Thomas* (New York: Noonday Press, 1962), p. 127.

[14] Vernon Watkins in his introduction to *Letters to Vernon Watkins,* p. 17.

CHAPTER 1.

[1] Cf. this opening to the first chapter in Luke (8–11), where Zacharias, the priest, offers incense upon the temple altar. The connection between the ritual sacrifice in this scene and the implied sacrifice in the first line of the sonnet should not be overlooked. Particularly relevant to this sonnet is the angel's annunciation to Zacharias, whose son John the Baptist is the forerunner of Christ in his birth as in his death.

[2] Cf. Lancelot Andrewes's use of "owl-light" in his sermon on the Nativity, Christmas Day, 1622: "*Vespertina,* the 'owl-light' of our reason or skill is too dim to see it by." See his "Ninety-Six Sermons," ed. by J. P. Wilson, *Library of Anglo-Catholic Theology,* 11 vols. (Oxford: John Henry Parker, 1841–1854), Vol. I, p. 254. Cf. also the use of "owl-light" in John Webster's *Duchess of Malfi,* Act IV, scene 2, l. 360.

[3] "The Litanie," *The Poems of John Donne,* ed. by H. J. C. Grierson, 2 vols. (London: Oxford University Press, 1942), Vol. I, p. 344.

[4] "The Book of the Resurrection of Christ," *Coptic Apocrypha in the Dialect of Upper Egypt,* ed. and transl. by E. A. W. Budge (London: Oxford University Press and British Museum, 1913), p. 180. See also *Apocryphal New Testament,* transl. by Montague R. James (Oxford: Clarendon Press, 1926), p. 183.

[5] The Hebrew name for mandrake, *dudaim,* is related to the noun *dodim,* 'love.' See Genesis 30:14–16; Song of Solomon 7:13. See also *Othello,* Act III, scene 3, l. 330.

[6] J. Rendell Harris, "Note on the Mandrake in the Fathers," *The Ascent of Olympus* (Manchester, Eng.: University Press, 1917), pp. 139–140.

[7] The mandrake image occurs in Shakespeare in the following plays: *Romeo and Juliet,* Act IV, scene 3, l. 37; *Antony and Cleopatra,* Act I, scene 5, l. 4; *2 Henry IV,* Act I, scene 2, l. 17; Act III, scene 2, l. 339; *2 Henry VI,* Act III, scene 2, l. 310. In Donne's poetry there are several references to mandrakes: "Song," l. 2; "Twicknam Garden," l. 17; "The Progresse of the Soule," ll. 160, 167, 175; "Elegie upon . . . Prince Henry," l. 54.

[8] The mandrake image occurs in *C.P.* (69), "The School for Witches" and "The Enemies." The first story appears in *The World I Breathe* (Norfolk, Conn.: New Directions, 1939), p. 183. The second story appears in *The Map of Love* (London: J. M. Dent, 1939), p. 43.

[9] Harris, "The Origin of the Cult of Aphrodite," *op. cit.,* p. 109.

[10] C. J. S. Thompson, *The Mystic Mandrake* (London: Rider, 1934), pp. 114, 116.

[11] J. G. Frazer, *The Fear of the Dead*, 3 vols. (London: Macmillan, 1936), III, 33.

[12] "St. Stephen and Herod," No. 22, *English and Scottish Popular Ballads*, ed. by F. J. Child (Boston: Houghton Mifflin, 1904), p. 40. See also "St. Stephen Was a Clark" in *Ancient English Christmas Carols*, ed. by Edith Rickert (London: Chatto and Windus, 1928), p. 123.

[13] In the Pseudo-Clementine literature there is a similar concept of ovigenesis:

> The wise men who are among the Gentiles, say that first of all things was chaos; that this through a long time solidifying its outer parts, made bounds to itself and a sort of foundation, being gathered, as it were, into the manner and form of a huge egg, within which, in the course of a long time, as within the shell of the egg, there was cherished and vivified a certain animal; and that afterwards that huge globe being broken, there came forth a certain kind of man, of double sex, which they call masculo-feminine.

"Recognitions of Clement," chap. xvii in "Gentile Cosmogony," *The Ante-Nicene Fathers*, 10 vols. (Grand Rapids, Mich.: William B. Eerdmans, 1951), Vol. VIII, p. 197. See also Jane Harrison, "The World Egg," *Prolegomena to the Study of Greek Religion* (New York: Meridian Books, 1955), pp. 625–628.

[14] Aristophanes, *The Birds*, ll. 692 ff. See also Harrison, *op. cit.*, p. 625.

[15] See Eric Partridge, *Shakespeare's Bawdy* (London: Routledge, 1947), p. 88.

[16] Cf.

> But the secret and symbolical hint was the harmonical nature of the soul; which delivered from the body went again to enjoy the primitive harmony of heaven, from whence it first descended; which according to its progresse traced by antiquity, came down by Cancer, and ascended by Capricornus.

Sir Thomas Browne, "Hydrotaphia or Urn Burial," *Religio Medici and Other Essays*, Everyman ed. (New York: E. P. Dutton; London: J. M. Dent, 1945), p. 125.

[17] John M. Robertson, *Christianity and Mythology* (London: Watts, 1910), p. 340.

CHAPTER 2.

[1] "Virgo, rosa, virginum, Tuum precor Filium," in *Ancient English Christmas Carols*, coll. by Edith Rickert (London: Chatto and Windus, 1928), p. 23.

[2] Thomas, *C. P.* (40).

[3] *C. P.* (4).

[4] See T. H. White, *The Bestiary*, Capricorn Books ed. (New York: G. P. Putnam, 1960), pp. 132–133. See also "Physiologus," *The Epic of the Beast*, transl. by James Carlill (London: George Routledge, n. d.), pp. 229–230.

[5] For the complete hymn see *The Hymns of the Breviary and Missal*, ed. by Dom Matthew Britt (New York: Benziger Brothers, 1952), pp. 188–189. See also Richard Crashaw's variations on this hymn, "The Hymn of St. Thomas," in *Carmen Deo Nostro*, ed. by J. R. Tutin (London: George Routledge, n. d.), pp. 109–111.

[6] Thomas Dekker, "The Pellican," *Four Birds in Noah's Arke*, ed. by F. P. Wilson (London: Oxford University Press, 1924), p. 164.

[7] *Richard II*, Act II, scene 1, l. 126; *King Lear*, Act III, scene 4, l. 77; *Hamlet*, Act IV, scene 5, l. 146.

[8] "Mother, white as a lily flower," *Ancient English Christmas Carols*, p. 68. "Nap" in l. 3 means "draught."

[9] Gerard Manley Hopkins, "Wreck of the Deutschland," *Poems of Gerard Manley Hopkins*, 3rd ed. (New York and London: Oxford University Press, 1948), p. 57.

[10] See the "embryological" poems for similar imagery in *C. P.* (1, 4, 6, 108, 110).

[11] The Jacob's staff image appears as "star-set at Jacob's angle," *C. P.* (43). "The long stick set alight" may also have been fashioned out of Balaam's parable in Numbers 24:17: "There shall come forth a star out of Jacob, And a sceptre shall rise out of Israel."

[12] Cf. "Rung bone and blade . . ." with the anatomical imagery in *C. P.* (4):

> That globe itself of hair and bone
> That, sewn to me by nerve and brain
> Had stripped my flask of matter to his rib.

Cf. also, Thomas's line to the following:

> . . . I will lay sinews upon you, and will bring up flesh upon you and cover you with skin, and put breath in you, and ye shall live.
>
> (Ezekiel 37:6–10)
>
> Thou hast clothed me with skin and flesh
> and hast fenced me together with bones and sinews.
>
> (Job 10:11)
>
> Thou hast bound bones and veins in me, fastened me flesh,
>
> (Hopkins, "Wreck of the Deutschland," p. 55).

[13] See Genesis 28:12 for Jacob's dream, and Genesis 28:15 for the covenant between God and Jacob.

[14] Crashaw, *Carmen Deo Nostro*, p. 99.

[15] *C. P.* (9)

[16] Richard Morris, *Legends of the Holy Rood*, Early English Text Society, no. 46 (London: Trübner, 1871), p. xvii.

[17] The poison which Socrates drank was not of the hemlock tree; it came from the hemlock herb, *conium maculatum*.

[18] See the Books of Adam and Eve (Apocalypsis Mosis 19:3) and the Book of Enoch 42:5 in the Pseudepigrapha of the Old Testament, 2 vols. (London: Oxford University Press, 1913), Vol. II, p. 146n.

[19] *C. P.* (15, 36, 37, 73).

[20] Lancelot Andrewes, "Ninety-Six Sermons," ed. by J. P. Wilson, *Library of Anglo-Catholic Theology*, 11 vols. (Oxford: John Henry Parker, 1841–1854), Vol. II, p. 146.

Chapter 3.

[1] Dylan Thomas, MS. (no title) dated May 13, 1933, in the collection of the Lockwood Memorial Library, University of Buffalo, Buffalo, N.Y. This MS poem is of particular interest not only because it has yielded two lines for the second sonnet but because it has three lines startlingly similar to the opening lines of Hopkins's "The Windhover." Thomas's lines are:

> I caught on a yard of canvas inch a wing,
> Kingfisher's, gull's swooping feather and bone,
> Goodnight and goodmorning of morn and sun.

[2] Andrewes, sermon on the Resurrection, April 12, 1612. See "Ninety-Six Sermons," ed. by J. P. Wilson, *Library of Anglo-Catholic Theology*, 11 vols. (Oxford: John Henry Parker, 1841–1854), Vol. II, p. 307. See also the part in this sermon on the paschal lamb, pp. 296–297.

[3] *The Travels of Sir John Mandeville* (London: J. M. Dent, 1928), pp. 20–21. "Invention of the Holy Cross," *The Golden Legend of Jacobus de Voragine*, transl. by Granger Ryan and Helmut Ripperger (New York: Longmans, Green, 1948), pp. 269–271.

[4] S. Baring-Gould, *Curious Myths of the Middle Ages* (London: Rivingtons, 1869), pp. 382 ff.

[5] C. G. Jung, *Psychology of the Unconscious*, transl. by B. M. Hinkle (New York: Dodd, Mead, 1931), p. 279.

[6] See Matthew 27:33; Mark 15:22; Luke 23:33; and John 19:17–18.

[7] *Golden Legend*, p. 210.

[8] William Wood Seymour, *The Cross in Tradition, History, and Art* (New York: G. P. Putnam, 1898), p. 85, n. 2.

[9] Miguel de Unamuno, *The Christ of Velázquez*, transl. by Eleanor Turnbull (Baltimore: Johns Hopkins Press, 1951), Section VIII, p. 69.

[10] *C. P.* (29).

[11] St. John Chrysostom, "Encomium on St. John the Baptist," *Coptic Apocrypha in the Dialect of Upper Egypt*, transl. by E. A. W. Budge (London: Oxford University Press, 1913), p. 341.

[12] *Othello*, Act I, scene 1, ll. 87–88.

[13] The late Dr. Helen Flanders Dunbar, in an interesting note in her *Symbolism in Medieval Thought* (New Haven, Conn.: Yale University Press, 1929), p. 161, n. 176, pointed out the coincidence between zodiacal signs and liturgical calendar:

> Christ was crucified while the sun was in Aries. The date of Good Friday each year is determined in reference to the first time when the moon is in opposition to the sun (i.e. full moon) *after* the sun enters *Aries*. Moreover Aries signifies Ram. Christ is termed the Lamb of God, the name conveying to English ears no sex significance; but it is to be remembered that Agnus is the male lamb, in other words a baby ram.

See also Longfield Beatty, *The Garden of the Golden Flower* (London: Rider, 1939), pp. 130–131; and C. G. Jung, *op. cit.*, pp. 419, 518.

[14] *C. P.* (2).

[15] James H. Breasted, *The Dawn of Conscience* (New York: Charles Scribner's, 1946), p. 109.

[10] E. A. W. Budge, *Osiris and the Egyptian Resurrection*, 2 vols. (New York: G. P. Putnam, 1911), Vol. II, p. 309. A more recent translation is available in *The Pyramid Texts*, transl. by Samuel A. B. Mercer, 4 vols. (New York: Longmans, Green, 1952), Vol. I, Utterance 478, pp. 173–174. The Pyramid Texts are a body of ancient Egyptian literature consisting largely of funerary and burial rituals, magical formulas against harm to the dead, religious hymns to the gods, prayers for the deceased king, and praise of the greatness of the deceased king in the other world.

CHAPTER 4.

[1] Lewis Carroll, *Alice's Adventures in Wonderland* (New York: Macmillan, 1940), p. 100.
[2] *Ibid.*, p. 101.
[3] Plato, "Ion," *Works of Plato*, transl. by Benjamin Jowett, 4 vols. in one (New York: Dial Press, n. d.), Vol. IV, p. 298.
[4] In his indispensable bibliography of Dylan Thomas's work, J. Alexander Rolph notes that Thomas was a reporter for the *South Wales Evening Post* in 1931 and 1932. J. Alexander Rolph, *Dylan Thomas: A Bibliography* (London: J. M. Dent; New York: New Directions, 1956), p. xi.
[5] Cf. the riddles in this sonnet to the questions asked of Job by the Voice in the Whirlwind (Job 38:4 ff):
> Where wast thou when I laid the foundations of the earth? declare if thou hast understanding. Who hath laid the measures thereof . . . ? Who can number the clouds . . . ?

Cf. also the questions asked by Taliesin in two of his poems in "Bardic Lore," *Poems from the Book of Taliesin*, ed. by J. G. Evans (Llandbedrug, Wales: Tremvan, 1916), p. 65:
> What was the greatest measuring done by hand?
> Who will measure Inferno?
> How thick is its covering?
> How wide is its entrance?
> How great its degree of cold?
>
> What waters flowed
> Over the people of Pharaoh? . . .
>
> What was the ladder's base
> When it was raised towards heaven?
> Who was the evening's guide
> From earth to heaven?

[6] Bishop Lancelot Andrewes, in his sermon preached on Christmas Day of 1618, allows himself a verbal display of brilliance in his comments on this divine paradox of the "*Verbum infans,* the Word without a word." See "Ninety-Six Sermons," ed. by J. P. Wilson, *Library of Anglo-Catholic Theology,* 11 vols. (Oxford: John Henry Parker, 1841–1854), Vol. I, p. 204.
[7] At first glance it would appear that Thomas is punning on the

name of Pharaoh-necko (Pharaoh the Lame), an Egyptian ruler mentioned in II Kings 23:29 and II Chronicles 35:20. However, since this sonnet is centered on the birth of Christ, "Pharaoh's echo" may very possibly refer to the edict of the Pharaoh in Exodus 2:22: "Every son that is born ye shall cast into the river," which is echoed in Matthew 2:16 when Herod "sent forth, and slew all the children that were in Bethlehem, and in all the coasts thereof, from two years old and under, according to the time which he had diligently enquired of the wise men."

[8] *A Guide to the Egyptian Collections in the British Museum*, preface by E. A. W. Budge (London: British Museum, 1909), p. 105.

[9] The companion of this obelisk, also called Cleopatra's Needle, is in Central Park, New York City. The pair of obelisks was erected by Thothmes III as a durable chronicle (echo?) of his reign.

[10] J. Alexander Rolph, *op. cit.*, p. xi: "Moved to London, 1933."

[11] In *C. P.*: "twelve winds" (41), "twelve-winded circles" (145), "twelve-winded marrow" (45), "twelve triangles of the cherub wind" (63).

[12] There are two Jamaican riddles about bamboo and a man in Archer Taylor's *English Riddles from Oral Tradition* (Berkeley and Los Angeles: University of California Press, 1951), pp. 201, 202:

[Question]   A man stan' up widout guts.
[Answer]   Bamboo.
[Question]   Tallest man in Kingston don' have any belly.
[Answer]   Bamboo.

[13] "The Cherry-Tree Carol," F. J. Child's *English and Scottish Popular Ballads*, ed. by Helen C. Sargent and George L. Kittredge (Boston and New York: Houghton Mifflin, 1904), stanzas 3–5, p. 98.

[14] For a full account of this episode see chaps. 8 through 20, pp. 42–47, in the Book of James (Protevangelion), *Apocryphal New Testament*, transl. by Montague R. James (Oxford: Clarendon Press, 1926).

The theme of Joseph's suspicion and the episode of the trial of Mary and Joseph form two pageants (xii and xiv) of the Coventry Cycle of mystery plays, where the harshness and coarseness of the proceedings border on the obscene.

[15] James Joyce, *Ulysses*, Modern Library ed. (New York: Random House, 1940), p. 20.

Chapter 5.

[1] "Jesu" is the vocative or oblique case; in hymns the possessive case is indicated as *Jesus'*. Thomas uses this form again in the "Ballad of the Long-Legged Bait": "Jesu's stream," *C. P.* (168). See *A New English Dictionary* (London: Oxford University Press, 1901), Vol. V, p. 573, for *Jesu*.

[2] See Father Mapple's sermon on the Book of Jonah in Herman Melville, *Moby Dick*, Modern Library ed. (New York: Random House, 1926), chap. IX, pp. 39–48. Especially recommended is the edition of *Moby Dick* ed. by Luther S. Mansfield and Howard P. Vincent (New York: Hendricks House, 1952).

[3] Hugh Latimer, *Sermons on the Card* (New York: Cassell and Co., n. d.), pp. 16–17, 27.

[4] See Donne, "Annunciation," in *The Poems of John Donne*, ed. by H. J. C. Grierson, 2 vols. (London: Oxford University Press, 1942), p. 319; Rainer Maria Rilke, "Annunciation to Mary," *The Life of the Virgin Mary*, transl. by C. F. MacIntyre (Berkeley and Los Angeles: University of California Press, 1947), p. 9; William Butler Yeats, "The Mother of God," *Collected Poems* (London: Macmillan, 1950), p. 281.

[5] G. F. Northall, *English Folk Rhymes* (London: Paul, Trench, Trübner, 1892), p. 130.

[6] Thomas may be punning on the term "angel sleeve," a very wide sleeve usually hanging from the shoulder.

[7] Cf. card imagery in the trial scene in *Alice's Adventures in Wonderland*, and Charles William's *The Greater Trumps* (New York: Pellegrini and Cudahy, 1950).

[8] St. Ephrem, quoted by Ernest Jones, "The Madonna's Conception," *Essays in Applied Psychoanalysis* (London: International Psychoanalytical Press, 1923), p. 321. St. Ephrem the Syrian (*ca.* 300–*ca.* 379) spent most of his life near Edessa in Asia Minor as a monk, writing many commentaries on the Bible and composing numerous hymns. He is best known for his Mariological hymns, which are considered an important contribution to Catholic dogma.

[9] Rilke, *op. cit.*, p. 9.

[10] "Dear Son, Leave Thy Weeping," *Religious Lyrics of the Fifteenth Century*, ed. by Carleton Brown (London: Oxford University Press, 1939), stanza VII, p. 2.

[11] Ernest Jones, *op. cit.*, pp. 290 ff.

[12] Thomas, lines from Poem Seventeen in 1933 Notebook, unpublished MS, Lockwood Memorial Library, University of Buffalo, Buffalo, N. Y.

[13] Cf. *C. P.* (4), (23), (35).

[14] *Moby Dick* (Modern Library ed.), chap. C, p. 436.

[15] *Ibid.*, chap. LXXVIII, p. 342.

[16] Sandor Ferenczi, *Thalassa: A Theory of Genitality*, transl. by H. A. Bunker (Albany, N. Y.: Psychoanalytical Quarterly, 1938), p. 48.

[17] Carl G. Jung, *Psychology of the Unconscious*, transl. by B. M. Hinkle (New York: Dodd, Mead, 1931), p. 245.

[18] Andrewes, "Ninety-Six Sermons," ed. by J. P. Wilson, *Library of Anglo-Catholic Theology*, 11 vols. (Oxford: John Henry Parker, 1841–1854), Vol. II, p. 397.

[19] An interesting connection between polar regions and angels (relevant to this sonnet, at least) may be seen in the names of two ships in Sir Martin Frobisher's Arctic expedition of 1576, the *Gabriel* and the *Michael*. See *The Three Voyages of Martin Frobisher*, ed. by Vilhjalmur Stefansson, 2 vols. (London: Argonaut Press, 1938), Vol. I, p. cii. Less specific, but still related to the angelic hierarchies, was the name of Captain James Cook's ship, the *Archangel*, bound out of Lynn, England, for the Spitzbergen regions in 1788. See William Scoresby, *The Arctic Regions*, abridged ed. (London: Religious Tract Society, n. d.), p. 175.

[20] Thomas has made use of salt and its cognates in other poems. See *C. P.*: "Adam's brine" (34), "The salt unborn" (35), ". . . the salt / Incising summer" (36), "my salt unborn" (37), "the salt sucked dam" (55). According to Ernest Jones, *op. cit.*, p. 122, salt is the symbol of procreativeness.

[21] Salt, exorcized and blessed, is put on the tongue of the candidate for baptism as a symbol of wisdom and incorruption. St. Augustine refers to this rite in his *Confessions:* "And I was signed with the sign of His Cross and seasoned with His salt . . ." See *Confessions of St. Augustine*, transl. by F. J. Sheed (New York: Sheed and Ward, 1949), Book I, chap. xi, p. 14.

[22] For imagery of ice, cold, and snow see Hopkins' "Pilate," *Poems of Gerard Manley Hopkins*, 3rd ed. (New York and London: Oxford University Press, 1948), no. 76, p. 117.

[23] Dante Gabriel Rossetti's "Lilith" [from his "Sonnets for Pictures"] is based on this legend: *Poems and Translations* (London: Oxford University Press, 1926), p. 146.

[24] Dante, *Inferno*, Canto IX; Milton, *Paradise Lost*, Book II, l. 611; Blake, *Tiriel*, Part VI, ll. 296–297.

[25] John Livingston Lowes, *The Road to Xanadu* (Boston and New York: Houghton Mifflin, 1927), p. 486, n. 64. Lowes cites Friederich Martens's *Voyage to Spitzbergen and Greenland* (1671) as the source of Coleridge's "slimy things."

[26] William Scoresby, *op. cit.*, p. 184. Scoresby takes note (p. 183) of several varieties of medusae in the seas around Spitzbergen:

> More than six or seven kinds of Medusae may be distinguished, among which may be named, Medusa pileus, and the purse-shaped, bottle-shaped and orange-coloured medusae.

[27] *Ibid.*, p. 185. Scoresby never subordinated his religious wonder of Providential wisdom to his wonder of Providential variety. In addition to recording the six or seven kinds of medusae, he also recorded in an astonishing series of cubic progressions, the probable number of medusae in the seas around Spitzbergen:

> The number of medusae . . . was found to be immense . .
> In this proportion, a cubic inch of water must contain 64; a cubic foot, 110,592; a cubic fathom 23,887,882; and a cubical mile about 23,888,000,000,000!

Lowes quotes this information (from Scoreby's unabridged *Arctic Regions* (I, 179) in his notes in *The Road to Xanadu* (p. 486, n. 64) to point out that Coleridge's line "And a thousand slimy things" was not an exaggeration. And since, in the fifth sonnet, Melville's whale and Coleridge's bear and Thomas's medusa find a polar rendezvous, it would not be irrelevant to mention Melville's knowledge of Scoresby's work. In their illuminating annotations to *Moby Dick* (pp. x, xiv), Professors Mansfield and Vincent list Scoresby's volumes among the books Melville had read.

[28] Alister Hardy, *The Open Sea*, Part I, *The World of Plankton* (London: Collins, 1962), p. 127.

[29] *Ibid.*, pp. 127, 128.

[30] Virgil, *Eclogue IV*, transl. by J. W. Mackail, Modern Library ed. (New York: Random House, 1934), p. 274.

[31] The theme of animals miraculously endowed with speech at the Nativity appears in a woodcut on a sheet of carols, published in 1701, headed "Christus Natus Est: Christ is born." The woodcut represents "the stable at Bethlehem; Christ in the crib, watched by the Virgin and Joseph; shepherds kneeling; angels attending . . . ; a sheep bleating, and an ox lowing . . . , a raven croaking, a crow cawing, a cock crowing above them, and angels singing in the sky. The animals have labels from their mouths, bearing Latin inscriptions . . . The cock croweth, *Christus natus est,* Christ is born. The raven asked, *Quando?* When? The cow replied *Hac nocte,* this night. The ox cryeth out, *Ubi, Ubi?* Where? Where? The sheep bleated out, *Bethlehem,* Bethlehem. Voice from heaven sounded, *Gloria in Excelsis,* Glory be on high." This description of the woodcut appears in William Hone, *Ancient Mysteries* (London: William Reeves, 1823?), p. 103.

[32] "The Nativity of Our Lord," *The Golden Legend,* transl. by Granger Ryan and Helmut Ripperger (New York: Longmans, Green, 1948), pp. 49–50.

[33] Samuel Taylor Coleridge, "The Destiny of Nations," *The Poems of Coleridge,* ed. by E. H. Coleridge (London: Oxford University Press, 1940), ll. 270–274 (concluding fragment), p. 148.

[34] *Moby Dick* (Modern Library ed.), p. 188.

[35] There is a weed called Sussex sea-straw which looks like a long dried straw of seaweed. Whether Thomas knew of such a plant, I do not know. The only work which lists a description of sea-straw is a two-volume edition of flora and fauna by James Petiver, an eighteenth-century botanist: *Gazophylacium,* 2 vols. (London: John Millan, 1764), Vol. I, p. 10. Thomas made frequent use of sea-plant imagery in his early poems, particularly in his "birth" poems.

[36] For similar imagery see Dylan Thomas, "In the Direction of the Beginning (fragment of a work in progress)," *Wales,* no. 4 (March, 1938), pp. 147–148. Much in this fragment suggests a common ancestry with portions of the fifth sonnet and the "Ballad of the Long-Legged Bait."

Chapter 6.

[1] The *Zohar,* which in Hebrew means "brightness," is a mystical commentary in eight parts on the Pentateuch, partly in Hebrew, partly in Aramaic. Its authorship, for many centuries a matter of dispute, is ascribed by modern scholars to a thirteenth-century cabalistic writer, Moses de Leon of Granada, Spain. During his lifetime de Leon claimed that the work was divinely revealed by Elijah to Rabbi Simeon ben Yohai in the second century A.D. After the death of de Leon his widow confessed that he had written the work himself. For a detailed account of the *Zohar,* see Dr. J. Abelson's introduction to the first volume of the *Zohar,* transl. by Harry Sperling and Maurice Simon, 5 vols. (London and Bournemouth: Soncino Press, 1949), Vol. I, pp. i–xxvii.

[2] The *Cabala* (or *Cabbala* or *Kabbalah*) is both a system of Jewish theosophy and a collection of writings which had their origins in the tenth century. The name is from the Hebrew *qabbalah,* meaning "tradi-

tion." The term is usually applied to a body of esoteric and occult writings of which the most important are the *Zohar* and the *Sepher Yezirah* or "Book of Creation." These are mystical works which offer, to the speculative mind, anagogical interpretations of Scripture linking the spiritual world to this world. To the practical mind it offers, through numerological values attached to letters, the secret of wresting power and energy from the spiritual world to be applied psychologically and physically to this world.

At least three English poets reveal the influence of the *Cabala:* Milton, Blake, and Yeats. Milton must have learned about it from his younger contemporary at Christ's College, Henry More; Blake's interest in the *Cabala* may have come from Cornelius Agrippa and Thomas Vaughn; and Yeats incorporated its mysteries into his poetry from a reading of A. E. Waite and MacGregor Mather's translation of Baron Knorr von Rosenroth's *Kabbalah Denudata,* or the *Kabbalah Unveiled.* Whether these mysteries ever reached Thomas is a matter of speculation. He had read Milton and Blake and Yeats; and the Waite and Saurat works were easily available to him.

[3] A few words from the glossary of terms in Volume I of the *Zohar,* which I list below, may illustrate the resemblance to Thomas's own use of these terms and the concepts they represent. Next to each term I have indicated, in parentheses, the sonnets in which such words and concepts appear:

Gan-Eden	Garden of Delight (10)
Gehinnom	Hell, or the fire of primordial darkness (6)
Letters	The primordial forms of all beings (7)
Lilith	Female night demon (5, 6, 7)
Maamar	A creative utterance, the hypostasis of the Voice (6)
Serpent	Evil inherent in the primordial darkness (3, 10)
Tree of Life	The point of departure of existence separating into individual souls (2, 7, 10)
Waters	The created universe (6, 7)
Voice	The instrument of Creation, the sum total of the letters, the original heavens (6, 7)
Green	Divine attribute of mercy (10)

[4] See illustration in Milton O. Percival, *Blake's Circle of Destiny* (New York: Columbia University Press, 1938), pl. facing p. 70.

[5] Denis Saurat, *Literature and the Occult Tradition,* transl. by Dorothy Bolton (London: J. Bell, 1930), p. 111.

[6] Hardy, *The Open Sea,* Part I, *The World of Plankton* (London: Collins, 1962), p. 95.

[7] "The mythological figures that crowd upon me . . . are innumerable; but I restrain myself, and select those that produce the proper pictorial effect." Goethe to Eckermann on the classical Walpurgis Night scene in the second part of *Faust,* from *Conversations of Goethe with Eckermann,* transl. by John Oxenford, Everyman ed. (London: J. M. Dent; New York: E. P. Dutton), p. 345.

[8] Hardy, *op. cit.,* p. 98.

[9] *Ibid.,* p. 94.

[10] See Ovid, *Metamorphoses*, transl. by Rolfe Humphries (Bloomington, Ind.: Indiana University Press, 1955), Book IV, pp. 90–93.

[11] William Blake, *Milton*, Book II, stanza 38, ll. 24–31.

[12] *Ibid.*, Book I, stanza 21, l. 34.

[13] Robert Burns, "Tam O'Shanter": "He screw'd the pipes and gart them skirl"; Goethe, *Faust:* "The bagpipe here unites them," Part I, l. 120.

[14] *A Catholic Dictionary*, ed. by Donald Attwater; 2nd ed., rev. (New York: Macmillan, 1954), p. 523.

[15] There is a similar theme in a mystery play of the Coventry Cycle, "Christ and the Doctors" or the "Dispute in the Temple." Christ discusses the nature of the Trinity with the learned doctors, and in answer to their questions explains the necessity of his "second" birth or Incarnation. See "Christ and the Doctors," *Ludus Coventriae*, ed. by K. S. Block (London: Oxford University Press, 1926), pp. 178–187. Cf. also Lancelot Andrewes: "Two natures He had, and so two Nativities. One eternal, as the Son of God; the other temporal, as the Son of Man" ("Ninety-Six Sermons," ed. by J. P. Wilson, *Library of Anglo-Catholic Theology*, 11 vols. [Oxford: John Henry Parker, 1841–1854], Vol. I, p. 285).

[16] Candle and man of wax images appeared in one of Thomas's stories published in *Criterion* in 1935 and reprinted in the *Map of Love* in 1939. The tone, atmosphere, and vocabulary are noticeably similar to the sonnet:

> Stiff and straight, a man of wax stared back . . . The candles must not be blown out, he thought. There must be light, light, light. Wick and wax must never be low. All day and all night the three candles, like three girls, must blush over my bed. These three girls must shelter me.

Thomas, "The Visitor," *Map of Love*, pp. 30, 34. Cf. wax images in Webster's *Duchess of Malfi*, Act IV, scene 1, stage directions before l. 55.

[17] She is mentioned once in the Bible (Isaiah 34:14) as *Lilith*, her Hebrew name; but various translations have deprived her of her identity. In the Authorized Version *Lilith* is translated as "screech-owl," in the Vulgate as "lamia," in Luther's version as *Kobold*, and in the Revised Version *Lilith* appears in the margin as a variant reading.

[18] A. E. Waite, *The Secret Doctrine in Israel* (London: William Rider, 1913), p. 86.

[19] *Ibid.*, p. 104.

[20] *Ibid.*, p. 276.

[21] The concept of the seven land masses and seas has its origin in Brahmanic mythology. In modern times the seven seas are designated as the Arctic, Antarctic, North and South Atlantic, North and South Pacific, and Indian oceans. Since Adam is the "salt Adam," the first voyager, he would know this elementary nautical fact.

[22] The *Zohar* records the belief that Lilith is the instigator of punishments, calling for the infliction of punishment every day. See A. E. Waite, *op. cit.*, p. 104.

142

[23] I remember the little flattened scrolls, inscribed with deprecations against Lilith and her retinue, pinned to window curtains and tacked over doors in my home when my sister was born. Every possible entry into the room where the mother is in labor is protected against Lilith's intrusion.

[24] The bagpipe-breasted hags, the suggestion of mutilation, and the atmosphere of a bloody, orgiastic rite in the sonnet have their origin in this manuscript excerpt from Thomas's notebooks:

> Eat till all's gone, drink to the dregs
> Before the ladies' breasts are hags
> Before the waxred breasts are hags
>   and the limbs are torn
>   and the limbs are worn.

MS, dated July 15, 1933, Lockwood Memorial Library, University of Buffalo, N. Y. After the July date there is another date marked "Jan / 36." Whether this indicates an amendment of the 1933 lines I do not know.

[25] There is a parallel between this obstetrical scene with night-hags in attendance and the scene of the *obstetrices* or midwives in certain Nativity plays. There is also a grisly prefiguration in this scene of the three Maries in attendance upon Christ in the Descent from the Cross.

CHAPTER 7.

[1] "An Alphabetical Devotion to the Cross," *Religious Lyrics of the Fifteenth Century*, ed. by Carleton Brown (London: Oxford University Press, 1939), p. 149.

[2] *C. P.* (4). The manuscript notebooks reveal Thomas's early preoccupation with the image of letters, printing, and Bible:

1. For Jesus though his death's a logogram (June 10, 1931?).
2. . . . what's not remembered is half the mortal lecture.
   (Who lectures but old God, a phantom rector
     A walking bible printed polyglot).

The second quotation is marked "Poem 38" with no date. My guess would place it in the 1933 notebooks. The "walking bible" is a probable ancestor of the "walking word" in the first sonnet.

[3] Cf. "book of trees" to "tree of words" in "The Visitation" in *The Map of Love*, p. 32.

[4] According to Jane Harrison the song of the sirens is followed by death. See *Prolegomena to the Study of Greek Religion* (New York: Meridian Books, 1955), p. 199.

[5] Andrewes, "Ninety-Six Sermons," ed. by J. P. Wilson, *Library of Anglo-Catholic Theology*, 11 vols. (Oxford: John Henry Parker, 1841–1854), Vol. I: (1) p. 160; (2, 3, 4) p. 168; (5) p. 170; (6) p. 173.

[6] Andrewes, Vol. II, p. 162.

[7] *Ibid.*, p. 180.

[8] *Ibid.*, p. 236.

[9] Andrewes, Vol. I, p. 141.

[10] *Ibid.*, pp. 216, 231–232.

CHAPTER 8.

[1] Thomas refers to Christ as "My Jack of Christ born thorny on the tree" in an earlier poem (*C. P.*, 15). In an unpublished MS poem, dated Sept., 1933, there is an undecided preference: "bride (Jack) of Christ." The use of Jack in the sonnet makes of Christ not a simple, common fellow but one who is common to all of us. There are other possibilities: Thomas may have known about the puppet called Jack a Lent (or Jack of Lent) which was set up on Ash Wednesday, pelted with missiles for the six weeks of Lent, and finally destroyed on Palm Monday. Although this ritual may have been the symbolic banishing of death or the winter season, it anticipates the beating, mocking, and crucifixion of another Jack on the Friday following Palm Monday.

Thomas may also have been aware of Hopkins's "Jackself" in the sonnet, "My own heart let me more have pity on," and "This Jack, joke . . . immortal diamond" from "That Nature is a Heraclitean Fire . . ."

[2] See the hymn "Stabat Mater Dolorosa" in *The Hymns of the Breviary and Missal*, ed. by Dom Matthew Britt (New York: Benziger Brothers, 1952), pp. 275j–277.

[3] Cf. ". . . the shrine of his world's wound" and "O let him/Scald me and drown / Me in his world's wound." "Vision and Prayer," *C. P.* (162, 165).

[4] Richard Crashaw, "Sancta Maria Dolorum," *The Poems of Richard Crashaw*, ed. by J. R. Tutin (London: George Routledge, n. d.), pp. 102–103.

[5] Whether Thomas made use of medieval spelling for a pun, I do not know. Perhaps he was aware of the spelling listed for *angel* in the New English Dictionary as *angle* from 1200 to 1300.

[6] Miguel de Unamuno, *The Christ of Velazquez*, transl. by Eleanor Turnbull (Baltimore: Johns Hopkins Press, 1951), Part One, Section VI, p. 10.

[7] Lancelot Andrewes, also aware of the geometry of the Cross, comments on Ephesians 3:18: "Of which love the Apostle when he speaketh, he setteth it out with 'height and depth, lenth and breadth,' the four dimensions of the cross, to put us in mind . . . that upon the extent of the tree was the most exact love, with all the dimensions in this kind represented that ever was." Lancelot Andrewes, "Ninety-Six Sermons," ed. by J. P. Wilson, *Library of Anglo-Catholic Theology*, 11 vols. (Oxford: John Henry Parker, 1841–1854), Vol. II, p. 180.

[8] Crashaw, "Upon the Bleeding Crucifix," *op. cit.*, p. 108.

[9] Cf. "Unsex me here" in *Macbeth*, Act I, scene v, l. 42. Cf. also "the unsexed skeleton" in James Thomson, "The City of Dreadful Night," *Poetical Works of James Thomson*, 2 vols. (London: Reeves and Turner, 1895), Vol. I, p. 140.

[10] Unamuno, *op. cit.*, Part Four, Section I, p. 119. See also Part Three, Section XXIV, p. 110. There is an almost incredible similarity between this sonnet and Unamuno's meditations on the Crucifixion.

[11] Lancelot Andrewes speaks of Christ as "The Physician slain, and of His Flesh and Blood a receipt made, that the patient might recover!" See Andrewes, *op. cit.*, Vol. I, p. 113.

Chapter 9.

[1] MS poem, dated April, 1930, Lockwood Memorial Library, University of Buffalo, Buffalo, N. Y.

[2] *C. P.* (36).

[3] *C. P.* (44).

[4] *C. P.* (72).

[5] *C. P.* (88, 89).

[6] E. A. W. Budge, *The Mummy* (London: Cambridge University Press, 1925), *passim.*

[7] See E. A. W. Budge, *From Fetish to God in Ancient Egypt* (London: Oxford University Press, 1934), p. 504. For a full description of the twenty-four hour watch of the resurrection festival, see pp. 505–513.

[8] A. Lucas, *Ancient Egyptian Materials and Industries* (London: Edward Arnold, 1934), p. 87.

[9] In the Egyptian Ramesseum or coronation drama, the central portion of which re-enacts the resurrection of Osiris, some priestly embalmers are masked as monkeys and others as wolves. See Theodor H. Gaster, *Thespis,* Anchor Books (Garden City, N. Y.: Doubleday, 1961), p. 396.

[10] The *ka*, or double, also meant image, genius, character, or disposition. The *ka* is, in the words of E. A. W. Budge, the "abstract individuality or personality endowed with all [man's] characteristic attributes. This abstract personality has an absolutely independent existence. It could move freely from place to place, separating itself from, or uniting itself to, the body at will . . ." See E. A. W. Budge, *The Book of the Dead* (New Hyde Park, N. Y.: University Books, 1960), p. 73.

[11] *Ibid.,* pp. xi–xii.

[12] Budge, *The Mummy,* pp. 465–466.

[13] St. John Chrysostom, "Encomium on St. John the Baptist," *Coptic Apocrypha in the Dialect of Upper Egypt,* ed. and transl. by E. A. W. Budge (London: Oxford University Press and British Museum, 1913), p. 347.

[14] J. G. Frazer, *The Golden Bough,* abridged ed. (New York: Macmillan, 1940), p. 325.

[15] *Ibid.*

Chapter 10.

[1] See Part III of the Introduction to this book, p. ix.

[2] Here we have (1) the vision of the millennial union of the serpent and the dove; (2) an echo of Matthew 10:16: "be ye therefore wise as serpents and cunning as doves"; and (3) the recollection of the conversation between Alice and the Pigeon in *Alice's Adventures in Wonderland* (chap. V).

[3] "And when Jesus beheld him, he said, thou art Simon the son of Jona: Thou shalt be Cephas [or Peter], which is by interpretation, A stone" (John 1:42).

⁴ See Matthew 14:28 and 17:27, and John 21:7–11.

⁵ In Messianic lore a great feast is promised the redeemed, on the Judgment Day, upon the huge fish Leviathan.

⁶ Tertullian, *De Baptismo, The Ante-Nicene Fathers*, ed. by Alexander Roberts and James Donaldson, 10 vols. (New York: Christian Literature Co., 1890), Vol. III, p. 669. The image of Christ as a fish is contained in a quotation describing Mary as a river in which "was born that unique and eternal fish Jesus Christ." See Robert Eisler, *Orpheus, the Fisher* (London: Watkins, 1921), p. 252, n. 3.

⁷ It is possible that Thomas might have known the story of St. Brandan. In that tall tale of a wonder voyage, St. Brandan and his seagoing Irish monks land on a huge fish which they mistake for an island, cook a meal (of fish) on it, and, returning to it much later, celebrate Resurrection Sunday on its hospitable back. There is also a description in that story of a fabled land in the middle of the sea, a Land of Promise, which bears a resemblance to Thomas's soaring garden.

⁸ Sir Philip Sidney, *Astrophel and Stella*, sonnet XIV.

⁹ Thomas may be punning on Paul's pun in his use of the word "peeled." In Philippians 3:2, Paul warns his followers in abusive and derisive words: "Beware of the dogs, of evil workers, of those who mutilate the flesh." The last phrase is Paul's mocking play on the Greek verb for circumcise, *peritome*. Paul uses the verb *katatome*, which suggests the more violent verb amputate or mutilate. Hence his warning against the "amputation party." (The King James Version uses the tame word "concision.") And, as always, Paul speaks from a position of superiority. He is, to use Thomas's verb, "peeled." "If any other man thinketh that he hath whereof he might trust in the flesh, I more: Circumcised the eighth day . . . an Hebrew of the Hebrews; as touching the law, a Pharisee" (Philippians 3:5). Neither his Benjamite lineage nor his Pharisaic observance of the law, nor his privilege as a Roman citizen kept him from being "peeled," almost flayed by those who stood against him.

Bibliography

THE POETRY OF DYLAN THOMAS

18 Poems (London: Fortune Press, 1934).
Twenty-Five Poems (London: J. M. Dent, 1936).
The Map of Love (London: J. M. Dent, 1939).
Deaths and Entrances (London: J. M. Dent, 1946).
In Country Sleep (New York: New Directions, 1952).
Collected Poems (London: J. M. Dent, 1952).
The Collected Poems of Dylan Thomas (New York: New Directions, 1957).

SUGGESTED READING

Dylan Thomas, *Letters to Vernon Watkins* (London: J. M. Dent and Faber and Faber, 1957).
J. Alexander Rolph, *Dylan Thomas A Bibliography* (London, J. M. Dent, 1956).
Henry Treece, *Dylan Thomas—'A Dog Among the Fairies'* (London: Lindsay Drummond, 1949).
Elder Olson, *The Poetry of Dylan Thomas* (Chicago: University of Chicago Press, 1954).
William York Tindall, *A Reader's Guide to Dylan Thomas* (New York: Noonday Press, 1962).

Index

149

"The School of Witches,"
131n. 8
"The Tree," 85
"The Visitor," 141n. 16
Thompson, C. J. S., *The Mystic Mandrake*, 19, 20
Tindall, William Y., 6, 10
Todi, Jacopone da, 96
Travels of Sir John Mandeville, legend of Adam's grave, 34
Treece, Henry, 2, 5, 6
Tschelitschew, Pavel, 92

Ulysses. See Joyce
Unamuno, Miguel de, *The Christ of Velázquez*, 37, 98, 99

Van Gogh, Vincent, 2

Venus, 125, 126
Vincent of Beauvais, 81

Waite, A. E., 75
Wales, Thomas's editorship of, 4
Watkins, Vernon, 8, 11
White bear, image of, 71, 72, 93

Yeats, W. B., 4, 56, 74; "The Circus Animals' Desertion," 7; "Lines Written in Dejection," 7; "Prayer for My Daughter," 7; "The Wild Old Wicked Man," 7

Zodiac, 22, 32, 33, 40, 41, 134n. 13
Zohar, 74–76, 139n. 1

P3